Community Building

COMMUNITY BUILDING

Values for a Sustainable Future

LEONARD A. JASON

PRAEGER

Westport, Connecticut
London

Library of Congress Cataloging-in-Publication Data

Jason, Leonard.
Community building : values for a sustainable future / Leonard A. Jason.
p. cm.
Includes bibliographical references (p.) and index.
ISBN 0-275-95872-8 (alk. paper)
1. Community. 2. Interpersonal relations. 3. Interpersonal communication. 4. Social interaction. 5. Community organization.
I. Title
HM131.J35 1997
307—dc21 96-53938

British Library Cataloguing in Publication Data is available.

Library of Congress Catalog Card Number: 96-53938
ISBN: 0-275-95872-8

First published in 1997

Praeger Publishers, 88 Post Road West, Westport, CT 06881
An imprint of Greenwood Publishing Group, Inc.

Printed in the United States of America

The paper used in this book complies with the Permanent Paper Standard issued by the National Information Standards Organization (Z39.48-1984).

10 9 8 7 6 5 4 3 2 1

To those unheralded citizens and activists
who are building a sense of community in every village, town, and city.

Contents

Foreword: Communication and Community Building ix
Mara B. Adelman and Lawrence R. Frey

Foreword: New Vistas for Community Psychology xiii
John Moritsugu

Preface xv

1. Society at the Crossroads 1
2. Four Vulnerabilities 7
3. A New Paradigm for Hope 25
4. Religion and Spirituality 53
5. A Sense of Community 71
6. Partnerships with Communities 89
7. Wisdom Traditions as Our Guide 101

Afterword: An Eco-Transformational Application: Bridging the Macro to the Micro 111
Patricia A. Fennell

Notes 115

References 125

Index 141

About the Author and Contributors 153

Foreword: Communication and Community Building

Communication and community grow in each other's shadows; the possibilities of one are structured by the possibilities of the other.

—E. W. Rothenbuhler

The Process of Community Involvement

What is it about the concept of "community" that compels the imagination of scholars, practitioners, and the public alike? The mourning for the death of community, coupled with rhetorical appeals for community from virtually all sectors of our society—from neighborhood watch groups to presidents ("It takes a village")—demonstrates the profound yearning for connection in our culture. But what is it that we have lost and are trying to reclaim?

Leonard Jason's book goes a long way toward answering this question. His tour of community—from philosophy to physics, from ecology to mythology, and from religion and spirituality to psychoneuroimmunology—reveals many of the values we appear to have lost along the way. His text adds an important voice to the collective body of literature that speaks to the longing for community in the postmodern era, when the forces of urbanization, industrialization, and technology make it seemingly impossible for people to connect meaningfully with others (see Bellah, Madsen, Sullivan, Swidler, & Tipton, 1985, 1991; Gergen, 1991; Meyrowitz, 1985).

Longing for community has always been a central theme of our collective psyche. In this culture there is a love-hate relationship with community; people wish to be both apart from and a part of others. Alexis de Toqueville, an astute observer of the cultural landscape, noted how "strange" Americans were—rabid about their individualism, yet amazingly, a country of joiners where voluntary associations abounded even as their members remained islands unto themselves. This tightrope between individualism and collective action cannot be negated in our visions of community. In part, the struggle for individualism is not merely ideological but also a response to saturation by social obligations and information overload. Sustaining meaningful ties thus also necessitates periods of seclusion and reflection. How revealing that one of the most eloquent spokespersons on the theme of community is the Trappist monk Thomas Merton, who lived much of his life in solitude.

Given the perceived chaos of the contemporary world, it is easy to romanticize the communities of yesteryear, seeking to build bridges to the past in the hopes of directing our future. But let's not forget how insulated many of those communities were, their members accepted only if they were of a certain race, religion, or ethnicity, and only if they followed strict rules of conduct. As Shafer and Anundsen (1993) remind us:

> As tightly knit and stable as most old-style communities were, they were also homogeneous, suspicious of outsiders, socially and economically stratified, emotionally stifling, and limited in opportunities for personal and professional development. So long as members belonged to the right ethnic, religious, or racial groups—or stayed in their place if they did not—and behaved within a narrowly defined set of parameters, they could count on strong communal support. But if they strayed too far outside the lines, their fellow community members might well shun or harass them. (p. 6)

In our contemporary multicultural world, these are clearly not the types of communities we wish to emulate. There simply is no single vision of community to behold; today the test of social connection has as much to do with creating a space for difference and dissent as it does with sustaining collective visions and values.

What is it then that can bind us together into the type of collective structure that Friedman (1986) calls "a community of otherness," where confirmation of others walks hand-in-hand with the struggle over ideas and principles? Leonard Jason makes a valuable contribution in identifying symbolic practices as the thread for weaving community. The psychological sense of community, where people feel emotionally connected, that Jason and others (for example, McMillan & Chavis, 1986) adopt is created and sustained in communicative practices. As we have argued, "Ultimately, community is a social construction, grounded in the symbolic meanings and communicative practices of individuals, that fosters meaningful human interdependence in social aggregates. . . . Communication is thus the essential, defining feature—the medium—of community" (Adelman & Frey, 1997, p. 5).

Leonard Jason identifies some of the grand symbolic practices—the myths, rituals, and customs—that can help develop a more robust sense of community and energize community members. Our sense of social connection is also woven just as tightly in the small, even mundane, communicative practices of everyday life: the daily salutations to the mail carrier, the monthly bingo game where the same stories are told over and over, and the small talk at the local check-out counter. It is in everyday talk, microlevel interactions, and even fleeting encounters that we weave together the communal cloth and provide a foundation for larger collective action. While concrete everyday communicative practices without grand rhetorical gestures are like threads without stitching, grand rhetorical gestures without concrete everyday practices are loose stitches that soon disintegrate.

Throughout this text, Jason provides us with many concrete examples of highly textured communities that attempt to weave together the various levels of symbolic practices. He mentions the work we have been doing for the past eight years on communication and community at Bonaventure House, a residential facility for people with AIDS (for a synthesis of this research program, see Adelman & Frey, 1997). People often assume that living together with a life-threatening illness would be a great equalizer and a common bond for residents that makes community easy to achieve. But facing mortality, coping with illness, and experiencing the continual loss of others can be a frightening and self-absorbing journey that makes connection extremely difficult. Amidst this fragile and poignant drama, stability is created and sustained through communicative practices that grease the communal wheel and provide a sense of meaning within chaos. Collective practices, such as the balloon ceremony, a bereavement ritual where residents gather together and simultaneously release colored balloons, signify both the release of the deceased from suffering and the letting go of someone unique and special. These rituals are highly visible anchors for communal life. But stability is also found in the more personalized exchanges, from taking a fellow resident to chemotherapy to sharing a pack of gum. It is embedded in the visual artifacts found in scrapbooks created for the house and personal possessions left to others after death—legacies for collective memory. And it is found in the gossip, protests, and arguments that bond residents in acts of solidarity as they "fight to keep warm" (Myerhoff, 1978).

The grand and ordinary practices at Bonaventure House also reveal something very important about the symbolic construction of community—that the tensions of every day life are never resolved but instead are massaged day by day. In that sense, community is never complete, never finished. Part of the problem that we face is the paucity of our symbol system for talking about community. We reference community as a noun, like some construction project that is finished when particular types of communication are practiced. But community is better referenced as a verb, as processual and continually in flux. We must never forget that it is *community building*, and this "ing" is often disorderly, rebellious, and messy.

The process nature of community means that while we have some traditional maps that provide well-worn paths for guiding this process, we must also generate new trails and discover innovative modes for connecting and affirming social ties. For example, the NAMES Quilt for people who have died from AIDS unites people in both remembering and re-membering. Quilting bees are resurrected from time-worn traditions as both social activity and social activism, as action and symbol. Even as the quilt is displayed on America's front lawn of the Washington Mall, friends and family are busy stitching new panels in a tent nearby.

In the course of everyday life, there are many opportunities for enhancing the psychological sense of community that seem to elude us. Jason's text helps us better understand some of the symbolic practices and values that can help create and sustain what is clearly a day–to–day communal journey.

—*Mara B. Adelman, Ph.D.*
Seattle University

—*Lawrence R. Frey, Ph.D.*
Loyola University Chicago

Foreword: New Vistas for Community Psychology

I am honored to provide a foreword to *Community Building: Values for a Sustainable Future*. The book is both pragmatically and theoretically useful to the field of community psychology. In the best traditions of the discipline, Leonard Jason asks us to consider the concepts and values that drive our interventions and then to act on the basis of these values. The book answers the two most asked questions of any interventionist in the community: What can you really do for the neighborhood?, and Why are you interested in doing these things?

Jason addresses the process of acting in the real world. He uses a multidisciplinary perspective to derive the values by which we should act. He reminds us of the strengths of wisdom traditions that have given us direction in the past and can provide us with a sense of direction for the future. Especially in times of great and rapid change, the evolution of cultures seems strained to keep up with the human needs for purpose and meaning. The complexity of the post-modern world is daunting. In facing these seemingly insolvable puzzles, Jason reminds us of the power of two human resources: our communities and our spiritual traditions. He explores the thesis that these two resources can reinforce each other and in turn provide the answers for the crises of our times. The community psychologist comes down on the side of affiliation and meaning, connection and purpose, rather than isolation and alienation.

The wisdom traditions of the world have contended with the importance of both community and perspective. Jason asks us to consider the salutary effects of these basic human endeavors. He envisions community psychology facilitating efforts to create social networks and coherence. His observations come from one who has been active and successful in community interventions. His programs are effective in bringing about positive and sustainable change. He has let us in on his secret ingredient: The interventions are driven by soul. Rather than focusing on the conflict between knowledge and wisdom, Jason challenges us to look at the transactions between the two. He argues that the combination of the two makes for transformational programming.

While the proposition seems at once controversial and obvious, the contradictory reaction may reflect the inherent conflict within our discipline. We are historically a discipline that respects the objective and the subjective, the norm and the variance, the philosophical and the psychophysical. Jason's programmatic results strongly support the advantages of a dialectical and transformational model in the building of communities.

Jason has given us what we have come to expect of him, a work that demonstrates a wide-ranging and systemic view, that presents a challenging premise and the data to support his thesis. I am reminded of Thomas Kuhn's admonishment that our paradigms both help and hinder our understanding of the world and that progress is measured by the development of constructs that better fit the data at hand. Jason's proposition moves us to a better fit. It is in line with the recent works of Robert Bellah (*Habits of the Heart* and *The Good Society*), Thomas Moore (*Care of the Soul* and *The Re-Enchantment of Everyday Life*) and Robert Kegan (*In Over Our Heads: The Mental Demands of Modern Life*). We are in search of new ways to understand and honor our old yearnings in present contexts. We are in search of a sustainable future. This work advances our discussion of what that might be.

—*John Moritsugu, Ph.D.*
Pacific Lutheran University

Preface

> Does this path have a heart? If it does, the path is good; if it doesn't, it is of no use. Both paths lead nowhere; but one has a heart, the other doesn't. One makes for a joyful journey; as long as you follow it, you are one with it. The other will make you curse your life. One makes you strong; the other weakens you.
>
> —Carlos Castaneda
> *The Teachings of Don Juan*

American society has been in an accelerated state of transition for the past few decades. In the 1950s, approximately 70 percent of American households consisted of a husband working and a wife caring for the children at home. Today, only 8 percent of households fit this model (Yankelovich, 1993/94). In addition, 72 percent of Americans do not know their neighbors well; 66 percent have never worked with others to solve community problems; and when asked what traits contemporary Americans are more likely to embody than Americans of the past, interviewees select adjectives such as "materialistic," "selfish," "phony," and "skeptical" (Patterson & Kim, 1993/94).

In this book I describe a series of vulnerabilities that help account for many of the serious problems facing contemporary society in industrialized countries, including high crime rates; homelessness; alcohol, tobacco, and other drug addictions; and a pervasive sense of isolation and alienation, even within communities that once nurtured and protected their members. Meaningful connections within historical, philosophical, and epistemological issues are also explored as a foundation for understanding what appears to have gone wrong.

We are well aware of the need to effect change, build on communities' strengths, and stem the waste created by our society's problems (Caplan, 1964). While we have made strides in knowledge and understanding and have attempted to translate our insights into better social conditions, some believe that the fabric of our society is ripping. Bellah, Madsen, Sullivan, Swidler and Tipton (1985) suggest that, for many individuals, the meaning of life has been tied to increasing income and status, yet few are satisfied with such utter self-absorption. The lack of more satisfying symbols and goals may be weakening today's society. Faced with the enormity of our problems, we must not only look critically at current approaches but also reevaluate the frameworks and values that drive these approaches.

In this examination we find that something vital is lacking: a true sense of belonging and connectedness within communities. Integral to understanding connectedness or community is the concept of "psychological sense of community" (McMillan & Chavis, 1986). Sarason (1974) originally defined this concept to mean a supportive network, a stable structure that one can depend on for psychological significance and identification. Sarason further stated that developing this sense of community is one of life's major tasks and should be the overarching goal of all community interventions. If loss of community or connectedness is indeed an underlying root of many modern problems, then appreciating and understanding the development of community might well contribute to the analysis of more specific problems and—better yet—their resolution.

An historical perspective, described in chapter 2, takes into account changes that have put society at risk for its current problems and provides a way to explore and eventually address these problems on a deeper level. According to Morgan (1942), people have lived throughout history in communal dwellings. It was within the village that people helped one another not out of charity but because it was the natural way of life. At times, village life was burdened with narrowness and provincialism; however, the strong positive features of mutual respect, shared goals, cooperation, and neighborliness provided nurturance and meaning. Morgan suggests that these communities fostered natural, spontaneous interpersonal relations that grew from mutual affection, customs, and traditions. In comparison, after the onset of the Industrial Revolution, modern societies began to feature formal organizations, contracts, and legislatures. Modern societies have greater individual freedom, but the cost has been a decline in human connectedness, community spirit, and neighborliness (McLaughlin & Davidson, 1985).

Over the past 150 years, sociologists and anthropologists have noticed a change in values within our culture. Prior to the Industrial Revolution, people had specific roles in crafts and farming, and these jobs provided meaning to their lives. As more people moved from the villages to the cities, severing long-term bonds with the land, family and community traditions began to weaken. Stein (1960) traced the effects of urbanization, industrialization, and bureaucratization on the transformation of America. He concluded that industrialization replaced a sense of coherence and satisfaction with one's craft with a new emphasis on prospering financially.

The Industrial Revolution marks a major shift in the experience of community for many people, but other forces may also have contributed to the reduction in sense of community. When societal and community norms, such as culture, rituals, and customs, weaken, people tend to lose their sense of coherence and their interest in community participation. Changing values and beliefs and the general loss of connectedness have corresponded with an increasing focus on the individual. In the 1940s and 1950s, there was a new dedication to an ever-rising standard of living, which justified the industrial work role. The local community ceased to be a place that mattered, and life transitions were minimized or performed perfunctorily by impersonal social agencies, schools, or churches (Stein, 1960). High levels of alienation and isolation occurred.

Spretnak (1991) offers a provocative set of propositions concerning vulnerabilities that occurred even before the Industrial Revolution. She believes that many maladies of our modern world are consequences of our tendency to try to dominate the forces of nature rather than to live in respectful balance with them. For Spretnak, a breakdown in the sense of community was inevitable once we started to consider the larger forces of nature to be engulfing and devouring and the ideal became self preservation and control. Finding a balance with nature by reducing pollution, controlling overpopulation, and preserving the land might give people the resources to nurture their communities. Through this redevelopment of a sense of community in balance with nature, we might ensure the survival of our species.

The Scientific Revolution has provided a valuable way to understand and improve the natural world, yet it may have shaken our sense of community. Although we can appreciate the enormous improvements in our world that science has made—for example, the sophisticated treatment of diseases and more efficient agricultural methods—the passion to understand and improve upon nature may have contributed to a crisis in values and belief systems. As science prospered, some began to believe that intellectual prowess and achievement were the only symbols of success (Bartel & Guskin, 1971). Others, including many existentialists (Sartre, 1956), proposed that religions and myths, which had once guided people through their lives, were antiquated and no longer relevant. Campbell (1949) maintains that many of our modern-day problems result from the decline of symbols, images, and myths as nurturing and validating rituals in our lives. This breakdown in a culturally transmitted sense of coherence and meaning may also have contributed to a reduction in our sense of community.

This book neither denies nor devalues the many contributions made by western civilization. Many people in urban settings have been able to integrate old and new traditions and to develop a sense of community. In addition, there are individuals in industrial societies who maintain the traditions, values, and myths that effectively guided their ancestors. However, many others in our mobile, industrial society lack a community of reference; the rich ties to their past belief systems and customs have been weakened. Thus we may need to take these factors into account in designing social and community interventions. Chapter 3 provides possible solutions to some of these problems, borrowing heavily from new developments in a variety of fields, including education, philosophy, and technology.

Smith (1994) has summarized some of the perils of post-modern selfhood, including the fading of religion as a moral guide and the wish to manipulate the external world for one's own personal ends. For many, the result has been a loss of hope, absence of community, and a loss of tradition and shared meaning. In chapter 4, I review eastern and western religions that hold traditions to which we may look for moral guidance and inspiration. The energizing symbols and messages of these faiths may be employed to restore a sense of shared meaning and to develop a more robust sense of community.

Ruth Benedict, Paul Radin, Meyer Fortes, and E. R. Leach explored cultures in which everyday life was imaginatively transformed and saturated with meaning (Stein, 1960). In these cultures life transformations were honored, and people lived their lives in balance with nature. Certainly, many people continue to guide their lives with the help of vital and energizing symbols and images. Many achieve a balance between modern civilized life and nature and maintain rituals and customs to help make life more meaningful and comprehensible. It is to these people that we should look for guidance on how to strengthen our connectedness to one another and to the world in a larger sense.

While it is essential to examine all of the elements necessary for the formation of healthy and nurturing communities, no such examination would be complete without concrete examples of how these elements are being used today to promote human well-being and social improvement. In chapters 5 and 6, I explore real-world models of community that effectively address some of today's devastating problems. These communities may not have surmounted all the problems of modern society, but they are working for their members in significant ways. The final chapters provide many such examples, from communities of healing to successful community-based interventions.

My hope is that present and future generations of helping professionals will look to the wisdom of the ancient past, the hard lessons of history, and the most innovative efforts of the present. It is in the synthesis of these three worlds that our greatest hope for the future resides.

This book provides a distinct analysis of problems faced by contemporary Americans and offers potential sources of solutions. Other books have presented more limited perspectives or analyses of these topics. For example, feminist theorists such as Charlene Spretnak (1991) have tended to focus on risk factors resulting from our attempts to dominate nature rather than to live with nature in an interconnected way. However, relevant psychological and sociological theories have been sometimes neglected in the feminists' work. Psychoanalysts have embraced the vulnerability that springs from our genetic animal ancestry. Community psychologists and sociologists have focused on the unintended consequences of the Industrial Revolution, including our loss of connection with the land and traditional crafts. The thesis of this book is that all of these vulnerabilities need to be conceptualized together if we are to undertake a comprehensive and thorough analysis of the factors predisposing our society to its significant social problems. This book is unique in its proposals for ecological and community-building interventions and for systemic solutions that extend beyond the focus on the individual that has increasingly been recognized as limited and ineffective.

The audience for this book includes concerned and educated Americans who are searching for a scholarly and cogent presentation of our present social difficulties and their predisposing factors. Another group of potentially interested readers are public policy officials and administrators who are seeking cost-effective and meaningful solutions to our ubiquitous social problems. Finally, readers with interests in mythology, religious experience, and philosophy will be particularly interested in this book because these topics are reviewed from a fresh perspective, one that shows how concepts from these domains can reenergize the search for a deeper meaning in life and the quest for more effective ways of honoring life transitions. Americans are increasingly interested in seeking solutions to our social problems. This book provides a synthesis of stimulating and thought-provoking ideas that could lead to these solutions.

I wish to thank the many people who have contributed to the formulation of many of the ideas expressed in this book. I am most appreciative of the constructive and valuable feedback I received from undergraduate and graduate students at DePaul University while writing this book. To my colleagues at DePaul University, including Sheldon

Cotler, Sheila Ribordy, Karen Budd, Kathrine Grant, LaVome Robinson, Rod Watts, Joseph Ferrari, Karen Jordan, Susan Dvorak McMahon, and Gary Harper, my thanks for their friendship and their unstinting support of my work. Other friends and colleagues, including Pat Fennell, Barbara Pino, Thomas Wolff, Mara Adelman, Lawrence Frey, Stevan Hobfoll, Laura Sklansky, Jennifer O'Hara, Susan Rosenthal, Lisa Belar, Julie Rosenberg, Sharon Cohen, Patricia Novak, Barbara Sommers, Jerry Walanka, Fred Friedberg, David Glenwick, John Moritsugu, Cliff Brickman, Arne Reichler, Jeffrey Messerer, Richard Katz, Jennifer O'Hara, Gretchen Otten, Olga Reyes, Anne Bogat, Jean Rhodes, Jean Hill, Doreen Salina, Roger Weissberg, Chris Keys, Dick Winett, Tom Gullotta, Joe Zins, Judith Albino, Maureen Minogue, Fabricio Balcazar, Yolanda Suarez, Joseph Durlak, Sonora Guldi, Marty Greenberg, Judy Richman, Andy and Sigita Plioplys, Bill McCreadie, Fred Rademaker, Emory Cowen, Edwin Zolik, Stephen Goldston, and Jim Kelly, were inspirational sources of support and guidance. From Barbara Sylvestri, Buzz Talbot, Donna Stein, Jim LeRoy, Dvorah Budnick, David Lipkin, Diane Allene, and Carole Howard, I learned the importance of creativity and collaboration when one is working on community change. From Beth Ferris, Verna Kragnes, Rick Hall, Darryl Eisenberg, and Steve Everett I experienced firsthand the healing capacities of hope and community building. From my family, including Jay and Lynn Jason; Diane, George, David, Johnathan, and Lisa Allen; Calvin Peltz, Sid and Joy Roth; Shirley and Mark Circus; Berry Levy; Sherry Kress; and Terri Foote; Edith and Allen Stern, Nancy and Adi Shatz; and Alvin, Sonja, and Joanna Wicks, I learned the importance of wisdom, humor, and patience.

I wish to thank the people at Praeger—particularly Marilyn Brownstein, Jean Lynch, Michelle Scott, and Nita Romer—for believing in this project. Harriet Melrose, Dana Clealy, and Meg Davis-Curtin were most helpful in editing several sections of this book. And finally, with elegance and imagination, Pam Woll did an extraordinary job of editing the entire book.

1

Society at the Crossroads

> Our eyes and ears are incessantly bombarded by a mythology which breeds greed, envy, pride, lust and violence, the mythology of our mass media.... An emotional deficiency disease, a paralysis of the creative imagination, an addiction to superficialities—this is the physician's diagnosis I would offer to account for the greater part of the widespread desperation of our time.
>
> —H. A. Murray (1959), pp. 607–608

OUR PROBLEMS

American society is confronted with numerous, seemingly insurmountable problems, including homelessness, AIDS, gang activity, and domestic violence. More and more people face battles with alcoholism and other substance abuse, and physical and mental illness. Mental disorders affect 22 percent of the population within a one-year period; 3 percent have severe mental illness, but only 20 percent of all mental disorders and 62 percent of severe mental disorders are treated within a given year (Regier et al., 1984; NAMHC, 1993). Seemingly safe and healthy communities are feeling the full force of these problems. Many people have suffered invasions of property or person. In 1990, 34.8 million Americans were victimized by crime (National Crime Survey, 1991). Individuals may try to ignore such encroachments in their lives, but the disintegrating social structure entangles even sheltered or isolated citizens. Communities try to mobilize against these problems, but individuals seem less connected, lacking direction and certainty about how to proceed.

Communities have high rates of divorce, alcohol and other drug abuse, homelessness, domestic and gang violence, and suicide. Marriage has become for many a disposable relationship, similar to entering into a rental agreement (Etzioni, 1993). Each year, more than a million children's families come apart through divorce (Levine & Perkins, 1987), often after years of conflict that have led to debilitating psychological and physiological distress. Twenty percent of American children drop out before they are eligible to graduate from high school (Parker & Asher, 1987), and some inner-city schools have dropout rates higher than 50 percent. More than two million children each year are subjected to abuse (American Association for Protecting Children, 1987), and three fatalities occur daily (Wurtele, 1993). Two million American children between the ages of 7 and 13 return home after school to empty houses, and 30 percent of children receive inadequate medical care (Zigler & Finn, 1982). Increased sexual activity has resulted in high rates of adolescent pregnancy, and teen parents face long-term economic and vocational challenges (Robinson et al., 1993). In addition, our nation's children spend more time watching television than engaging in any other activity except sleep, and the images they see are filled with high levels of violence and sexuality (Jason & Hanaway, 1997).

The gap between the rich and the rest of us continues to grow: 1 percent of Americans own 40 percent of the national wealth; and between 1977 and 1989, families with incomes higher than $350,000 received 72 percent of the country's income gains (Dugger, 1995). Such disparities in income are bound to lead to increasing social tensions. In addition, many who have jobs fear being let go due to corporate downsizing.

Health care costs are increasing, and this places additional burdens on communities. In 1992, 14 percent of our nation's total economic output ($830 billion) was directed to the health care system, whereas in 1965 health care expenses accounted for only 6 percent of the total economic output. If the health care system is not improved, by the year 2000 the costs are expected to double, and an estimated 39 million people will be uninsured.

Other assaults to health include the lack of clean water, fresh air, sunlight, unprocessed food, and exercise. Contemporary diets, lifestyles, and farming practices have predisposed us to heightened risk of disability and premature death. Schmid (1987) reviewed the diets of traditional people who grew vegetables without pesticides; raised beef, chicken, and pigs without chemicals and hormones; and hunted wild game. These people were largely free of hypertension, heart disease, arthritis, colitis, obesity, diabetes, cancer, and stroke. These devastating illnesses are prevalent in industrial societies in part because of diets that include processed foods dangerously high in fats, salt, and sugar. Historically, the cause of the demise of many great civilizations has been topsoil depletion, and

75 percent of the original U.S. topsoil has already been lost. In addition, the widespread use of chlorinated hydrocarbon pesticides is the principal reason for sterility and the reported sperm count reduction in U.S. males.

Changes in our ecosystem have been linked to rapidly expanding populations of bacteria, parasites, and viruses. Robbins (1987) cites data indicating that 55 percent of antibiotics used in the United States are added to livestock feed and that this has led to the breeding of antibiotic-resistant bacteria in factory farms. For over 50 years, we have increasingly relied on antibiotics to treat a wide variety of health problems—even conditions where antibiotics are not effective (for example, viral infections such as the flu). Bacteria reproduce so quickly (every 20 minutes) that the 50-year time span during which antibiotics have been used is equivalent to 18 million years of human evolution. During these 18 million evolutionary years, new strains of bacteria have adapted to the changes that antibiotics produce in their host environments. Some strains are now resistant to all antibiotics, but these bacteria are currently of the non-deadly type. If deadly bacteria become resistant, our over-reliance on the use of antibiotics will have contributed to a catastrophe of unimaginable proportions.

Physical changes in ecosystem structure have also had negative health consequences. For example, as forests are cleared and more individuals move to formerly wooded areas, people are now coming into more frequent contact with the ticks that carry Lyme disease. Tick populations have increased dramatically because the deer that carry them have proliferated due to the extermination of their natural predators.

Even more ominous is the greenhouse effect, caused by a build-up of carbon dioxide from automobile emissions and the burning of oil and coal. When the sun's rays enter the earth's atmosphere, greenhouse gases prevent them from escaping back into space, thus increasing the temperature of the earth's atmosphere. Some have projected that by the year 2050, our planet will have increased in temperature by four to five degrees. The resulting expansion of the oceans and melting of the polar ice caps would raise the sea level high enough to flood many currently inhabited areas. Cape Cod, Florida, and Louisiana might become flooded. Clearly, we have not been wise guardians of our precious resources.

The issues reviewed above include both contributors to and reflections of the breakdown in community that we are witnessing. What is clear is that many vulnerable groups within our country are daily exposed to poverty, illness, exploitation, and prejudice (for example, millions of migrant farm laborers, unemployed casualties of corporate downsizing, poverty-stricken elders, and unemployed inner-city teenagers) (Albee, 1996). If we are to be successful at reducing physical illnesses and preventing mental disorders, we will need to direct more of our efforts toward building sturdier and more vibrant communities.

ATTEMPTED SOLUTIONS

We stand at a crossroads, and the dominant political factions seem incapable of providing feasible solutions to ubiquitous societal, community, social, and personal problems. Liberals who espouse larger social and government programs to remediate these problems must contend with a growing conservative backlash and federal deficits. A majority of citizens are increasingly dissatisfied with underwriting government programs that both increase taxes and provide disincentives for joining the workforce, and there is little support for large-scale redistribution policies. Welfare programs are perceived as creating a culture of dependency. Clearly there is a need for a new social agenda with symbols and vitality that can transcend the polarities that threaten to disrupt our nation. This agenda must reach back into the historical and cultural influences that have shaped our society and forward into the vision of a future that affords safety and dignity for all.

When psychologists mount efforts to improve people's lives, their efforts are usually directed toward reforming the status quo rather than radically altering it (Fox, 1993). Even when liberals succeed in bending the law in a more humane direction, people often begin to seek solutions to community problems through the legal system, which reduces their ability and motivation to work together and develop a sense of community. Fox (1993) suggests that we may need to refocus our attention from the law as the reservoir that holds solutions to our human problems and instead begin to identify our values through new sources, such as psychological theory and personal ethics.

We are thoroughly immersed in the Information Age, in which new inventions and devices are intended to make our lives better and more satisfying. For many people, this revolution has instead made their lives more complicated and less enjoyable. In spite of modern technology, people have little time for relaxation, enjoyment, and contemplation.

In their well-received book *Habits of the Heart*, Bellah, Madsen, Sullivan, Swidler, and Tipton (1985) claim that, as social interactions have become more intense, limited, and transient, the individual has become the only firm reality. The meaning of life has become tied to the acquisition of ever-increasing income and status. Rather than looking for ways to make our lives more fulfilling and meaningful, we focus on consumption and profits, and as a consequence we are surrounded by information and symbols that are either irrelevant or devoid of meaning (Slama, 1993). These symbols and the goals of consumption and profits are often explicitly adopted by the leaders of political parties and social institutions. However, few people are genuinely satisfied living lives devoted to ambition and consumerism.

Futurists have identified six long-term worldwide trends in social structures: proliferation of technology (for example, automation, robotization); increasing and shifting population (for example, rapid growth in third-world countries and increases in minority and elderly groups); changing economic growth and development (for example, widening gaps between the rich and poor and exploitation of natural resources); expanding communication and power dependent on the control of knowledge; changing social expectations (for example, gender equalization and new family patterns); and shifts in belief systems (for example, declining traditions in some regions and a resurgence of fundamentalism in others) (Sundberg, 1985). This book focuses on this last issue, the uncertainty about norms and values.

A PSYCHOLOGICAL SENSE OF COMMUNITY

This book proposes that some of the solutions to society's problems may be gleaned from other cultures. For example, Arrien (1993) provides evidence that in solving personal and community problems, indigenous people have frequently used four archetypal paths: those of the warrior, the teacher, the healer, and the visionary. The path of the warrior teaches the use of right power in leadership, solving problems by being reconnected with the creative fire within ourselves. The path of the teacher communicates meaning, gratitude, and acknowledgment; these teachings from the heart help us reclaim our authentic selves and inhibit our ability to feed our false-self systems. The path of the healer requires listening to the guidance within. The healing of soul loss might best be viewed as an attempt to understand why we have stopped singing and dancing and why we have become uncomfortable with the sweet territory of silence. Finally, the path of the true visionary depends on a regenerative capacity to dream and see in other dimensions and to use imagination unfettered by the constraints of old paradigms. These metaphors may be abstract, but they point to truths that can be enormously helpful in healing the systemic wounds that confront twentieth-century civilizations.

In this book I explore anthropological, historical, philosophical, religious, and epistemological explanations for the decline in sense of community and the subsequent emphasis on individual goals as a source of meaning. Implications for our society are highlighted, and possible alternative models for healing our problems are reviewed. These models are illustrated in the final chapters with examples of healing communities and community-based interventions.

To begin this exploration, in the next chapter I examine four vulnerabilities that predispose industrialized societies to unacceptable levels of individualism and a breakdown in the psychological sense of community.

2

Four Vulnerabilities

One disease, long life, no disease, short life.

Those who take care of themselves accordingly will tend to live a lot longer than those who consider themselves perfectly healthy and neglect their weaknesses . . . a weakness of some sort can do you a big favor, if you acknowledge that it's there.

—Benjamin Hoff
The Tao of Pooh

SIGNS OF DECAY

Many will disagree with the analysis of our country presented in chapter 1. Some economists point out that ecologists' predictions about dwindling natural resources have failed to take into account that new technologies allow us to identify more efficient ways of using our natural resources. They also point out that we won the Cold War against the Soviet Union, and that the United States has replaced Japan as the most competitive country in the world market. The workplace is safer than it was 25 years ago, and crime and divorce rates are dropping. Women are making impressive strides in the workplace, there are fewer high school dropouts, and the majority of Americans pray regularly (Ladd, 1993/94). Diener and Diener (1995) cite data demonstrating that most people report positive levels of subjective well-being, indicating that they are not elated but are at least mildly happy and satisfied in domains such as marriage, work, and leisure. How might these optimistic and promising developments be reconciled with the more depressing issues reviewed earlier?

Perhaps both sets of facts have some grounding in reality. Our country has much to be proud of, and it is the envy of nations throughout the world. However, beneath this prosperous exterior there are troubling signs of decay in the sense of community and family life. This chapter explores four vulnerabilities that may help account for the problems that confront our nation. They are aggressive tendencies within our genetic makeup, separation from nature, loss of external symbols and guideposts, and separation from the land. To some these might seem like four strengths, for they have been so regarded by many who have shaped our culture's evolution. These factors destroy more than they yield, however. They ultimately separate us from our true nature and our true sense of community, in which our potential for personal, social, and cultural healing resides.

This chapter is the story of our fall from grace, our entry into the wilderness described in the previous chapter. The four vulnerabilities establish a foundation for the model of community healing presented in the remainder of the book.

AGGRESSIVE TENDENCIES IN OUR GENETIC MAKEUP

A function of our genetic animal ancestry, the first vulnerability—aggression—has been with our species from our most primitive days on this planet. The age of the hunter comprises from 95 to 99 percent of our history (Lorenz, 1974). In Konrad Lorenz's book *On Aggression*, violence is depicted as a deeply rooted part of our behavior. The aggressive, competitive libidinal animal tendencies within human beings have been studied by many prominent psychologists and psychoanalysts and made most familiar in the writings of Freud.[1] Some aggressive tendencies are genetic but are normally controlled by culture to avert self-destructive behaviors. If self-regulating mechanisms break down, then people become more aggressive. On the other hand, there is equally persuasive evidence that the will to form alliances for mutual well-being is also written into our nature as human animals. The following pages explore the delicate balance between these two natural tendencies, and what has happened to that balance as our species has evolved and allowed our competitive urges to overwhelm our cooperative instincts.

Human beings and chimpanzees, our closest animal relatives, have 98 percent of their DNA in common (Cavalieri & Singer, 1994). Jane Goodall's work with chimpanzees at Gambie has provided interesting clues about the ancestors of our species. These bright animals can make and use primitive tools. For example, Goodall observed chimpanzees poking leaf stems into termite mounds, and when the termites clung to the leaf stem, the chimps had a nutritious meal.

Chimpanzees live in communal groups for protection and support; they are protective of their children, providing them with food and safety. It is also part of human nature to establish enduring reciprocal alliances of friendship and to direct altruism toward kin (DeKay & Buss, 1992). Dreher (1995) suggests that helping behaviors actually result in a biochemical reward, via the release of endorphins, creating an incentive to help again and again. Like dominance urges, helping tendencies may be embedded in the brain structure. It is also likely that chimpanzees' abundant energy, playfulness, and vitality are characteristics that reside naturally within human beings, and that these vibrant inner resources can supply the fuel for an animated and spirited life.

Like human beings, chimpanzees are burdened by aggression. Before Goodall's work, they were considered completely vegetarian and non-aggressive toward other animals. However, Goodall observed tribes of chimpanzees systematically killing members of other groups and aggressively protecting their territory. Often a dominant chimpanzee would act aggressively to show others that he was at the top of the social hierarchy. Some of these aggressive animal tendencies reside within our genetic makeup as well and can lead to vulnerabilities in our efforts to live in a civilized world. From an evolutionary, psychological point of view, possible reasons for these tendencies in human nature include competition for limited resources, concepts of property, urges toward retaliation and revenge, weapon making and using, and coalitions that use weapons for war (DeKay & Buss, 1992). Continuous wars reflect aggressive and territorial tendencies in our species. These instinctual tendencies put people in conflict with their social and humanistic needs for affiliation and community.

Thus, our most primitive vulnerability is the residue of our primordial animal past: our need to climb to the top of the hierarchy, by whatever means we have at our disposal, to reap the rewards of status, power, and resources. While these aggressive tendencies are adaptive in the non-human animal world, they have stimulated humans to expand their population and appropriate territory. As a result, the survival of all species is now threatened. If not carefully regulated by culture, rituals, and customs, aggressive tendencies can seriously interfere with our efforts to live together as families and communities. The high levels of unethical aggression in business may be in part a reflection of these primitive urges, no longer restrained by societal and community norms.

Our species is capable of horrendous behaviors, as evidenced by the Roman gladiator games in which people were forced to fight to the death for others' amusement, and the genocide practiced by the Nazi regime in Germany. In their social psychology experiments, American psychologists Stanley Milgram (1963) and Phillip Zimbardo have shown that "normal" people will give severe electrical shocks to innocent subjects when firmly instructed to do so, and that they will treat people inhumanely when instructed to take on the role of a prison guard (Heney, Banks, & Zimbardo, 1973). Clearly our settings and the prevalent values within them have strong shaping influences on our behavior. A key question is whether there has been a breakdown in some of our protective cultural guideposts and regulatory mechanisms, and it is to our primitive past that we once again look for clues.

OUR SEPARATION FROM NATURE

Change in nature is natural and constant. Current scholarship suggests that the evolution of hominids alone has taken at least three million years (Johanson & Shreeve, 1989). Through that period, these species slowly adapted, forming new relationships with their environments.[2] Walking erect, Australopithecus was able to spot both enemies and prey on the grassy African plains. Homo habilis, now considered the first primitive human being, developed the first rudimentary tools, marking the dawn of human technology. Homo erectus had a tall, powerful body and was able to travel quickly and easily, carrying meat from carcasses over long distances. The discovery of fire allowed this species to stay warm and frighten away predators. As these developments suggest, change is not necessarily a negative thing; however, some types of changes can have negative consequences. A feature of the western culture that has become dominant in the world is a tendency to control nature rather than to live in a respectful balance with her. A historical analysis documenting this tendency will be explored in this section.

Homo Sapiens

Homo sapiens emerged by around 32,000 B.C. (some claim as early as 100,000 years ago) and spread throughout the world. Less massively built than its predecessors, Homo sapiens was more efficient in planning and finding food. Its physical features approximated those of modern human beings. Their larger voice boxes allowed them to utter more distinct sounds than those of their ancestors. They developed complex languages that enabled them to pool their skills and efficiently pass them on to their children. They made weapons from sharp stones, they created sculptures, and their world was filled with sacred places. In Africa, Europe, Asia, and Australia, the emergence of Homo sapiens brought about a cultural explosion, one that set humans apart from the ancestors who had come and gone before (Wilber, 1995). The religious life of primal Homo sapiens' societies was polytheistic, and their deities were associated with the forces of nature (Livingston, 1989). Robert Ornstein, in his book *The Evolution of Consciousness,* says that our biological evolution ended with the appearance of language and speech; however, the world to which our biology adapted has vanished.

When Homo sapiens entered new lands—for example, Australia, Hawaii, and the Americas—many animal species became extinct. This was probably due both to climatic changes at the end of the last Ice Age and to our increasing prowess in hunting animals. For example, after Homo sapiens entered the Americas about 11,000 years ago, more than 70 percent of all species of animals weighing more than one hundred pounds became extinct (Wilber, 1995).

What role has our attitude toward nature played in our choice of behavior toward other species? Wilber (1995) asserts that some indigenous cultures have treated other species and the land itself in ecologically unsound ways; for example, using slash-and-burn agriculture. Wilber holds that a belief in the sacredness of nature does not guarantee an ecologically sound culture. Some early cultures showed disrespect toward the land and nature and eventually collapsed. However, in many early cultures, according to Campbell (1980), animals and Homo sapiens lived in an interrelated and interdependent world, where balance and respect for nature were essential parts of the way societies interacted with their environments.[3] In general terms, the thesis of this book departs from Wilber's analysis. I suggest that a more reverent attitude toward nature and a perspective that includes her sacredness did and still does help nurture a more ecologically sensitive way of being in the world.

Agriculture and the Goddess

From 9500 B.C. on, a great transformation took place as humans began to manipulate nature through agriculture and animal husbandry (Campbell, 1980). Our impulse to control nature led to the agricultural revolution (Upshur, Terry, Holoka, Goff, & Lowry, 1991). Horticultural agriculture was based on the use of a hoe or a simple digging stick. About 80 percent of foodstuffs were produced by women, who could safely use a hoe or digging stick even during pregnancy. The men continued to hunt animals. However, these new methods of farming sometimes exhausted resources in the forests and fields; some early villages failed when the land became barren and no longer provided enough food for their people.

In this planting world women gained importance, because they could plant, harvest, and rear the children. About one-third of these societies had only female deities, and about one-third had both male and female deities (Wilber, 1995). The farmers were polytheistic; they worshiped the forces of nature, including the earth, the sun, and the sky. According to

Campbell (1990), the mythologies of agriculture-based societies tended to suppress individualism; instead, people were persuaded to identify with norms and behaviors developed in the public domain. Rigid rules were necessary for the establishment of orderly settlements, and they were imposed on people who had previously been used to the freedom and independence of living in hunting and gathering societies.

Stone (1976) proposes that, during this time, goddess-oriented societies perceived the earth as sacred and that in these societies women and nature were respected. The people who worshiped the goddess lived in Old Europe, the Middle East, Asia, Africa, and the Americas. Some archaeologists place the beginning of goddess-oriented societies in the Neolithic communities of 7000 B.C.; others place it in the Upper Paleolithic cultures of 25,000 B.C. Some archeological findings from these communities indicate that the sexes were treated equally. According to Spretnak (1991), matrifocal societies had greater senses of honor, both for the earth-body and for the personal body. The divine was laced throughout one's existence; rather than focusing only on cultural achievement, people expended more effort to embrace life as a dynamic and creative process. Stone (1976) states that during this period women were viewed as givers of life. They were revered and deified and occupied a prominent role in society. Sex was sacred, a symbolic magic to invoke fertility in vegetation, livestock, and humans.

The female deities of this period do not simply represent fertility and the nurturing powers of mother earth, according to Livingston (1989). The mother goddess was pregnant with life and virginal, she was chaste and promiscuous, she created and destroyed, she unified life and fiercely divided it by conflict. She symbolized the duality inherent in life.

Paradise: Balance and Oneness with Nature

About 3000 B.C., horticultural farming was transformed into agrarian farming, which was based on animal-drawn plows that could not be handled by pregnant women due to the risk of miscarriage. Wilber (1995) believes that the agrarian revolution led to a massive shift in culture, with virtually all foodstuffs being produced by men. It is perhaps not coincidental that during this period the deity figures became almost exclusively male.

Agrarian farming was more economical than hunting and gathering, and soon more food was available for the expanding population. The food surpluses allowed a greater number of people to begin pursuing new cultural endeavors (Wilber, 1995). Attempts to understand the order of the natural universe led to the development of religion and philosophy.

A fundamental balance with the land was a key feature of many of the civilizations that began appearing throughout the world from 4000 to 2000 B.C. (Wood, 1992). These ancient civilizations attempted to understand and control the workings of their world (Upshur, Terry, Holoka, Goff, & Lowry, 1991). One example is Old Mesopotamia, a civilization that emerged upon the fertile banks in the confluence of the Tigris and Euphrates rivers about 3500 B.C. As cities rose from the land, increasing specialization led to the development of writing, mathematics, and astronomy. These ideas reached the Nile (and inspired the First Dynasty of Egypt) around 2800 B.C., the Indus Valley around 2600 B.C., China around 1500 B.C., and Peru (by way of the Pacific) perhaps as early as 1000 B.C. (Campbell, 1990). As early peoples observed the planets moving at a constant rate, they hypothesized that order and balance were essential properties of the universe. Their myths stressed that when people lived in accord with nature, nature would give its bounty to them (Campbell, 1980). These traditions depict a relationship of unity with the forces of nature, an integration of the different aspects of the self, and a reverence for all components of nature—both its light and dark aspects.[4]

From Duality to Dualism: The Fall from Grace

Our species had originally been firmly rooted in the animal kingdom, an integral part of nature. As if emerging from a massive mountain of rocks, we slowly became aware of our world in a way quite different from that of other animals. It is not that other animals do not have feelings or cannot solve problems; what differentiated us was the use of our brains to achieve mastery over the natural environment and to reflect upon our unique condition. As we evolved and began to exert more influence over our environment, our increasing consciousness of the natural world inevitably led to two opposite ways of being in the world. Many ancient cultures used this awareness to sanctify and appreciate their interconnectedness with the land and other animals.[5] Others gradually repudiated their link with the animal world, a world seen as wild, dangerous, and in need of being controlled. Our species had a critical choice: to remain aligned with, or to separate from, the natural world. Those cultures that defined themselves as apart from nature have become the dominant powers in the past four hundred years. The ascendancy of these cultures has led to spectacular scientific discoveries, which further consolidated the second vulnerability: separation from nature. A historical analysis follows that attempts to depict more closely this separation that we have identified as our second vulnerability.

According to Spretnak (1991), in East Central Europe, Indo-European and Semitic invasions destroyed the goddess-oriented civilizations, as three waves of horse-riding nomads migrated from the Eurasian steppes between 4400 and 4300 B.C., between 3400 and 3200 B.C. and again between 3000 and 2900 B.C.[6] Many of the Aryans did not negate the goddess; they merely placed her below their male gods. However, the goal of many of the new male-dominated religions was to transcend nature and the flesh (Graves, 1966). Spretnak (1991) believes that this shift from a religion centered on the goddess to an Indo-European-Greek religion—whose gods were remote, up in the sky, and warlike—is well established. Because, in this religion, the larger forces of nature were believed to engulf and devour humankind, the sense of connection between human nature and the rest of the natural world was broken, and human beings had to focus on self-preservation and control. For if everything is unconnected in a competitive world, then the logical response is to protect oneself by controlling as many other people and species as possible. This warrior society was dominated by men, and women were considered the property of men. The warriors brought with them the concept that light was good and dark was evil. The female deity became associated with darkness and evil; the male deity became the champion of light. The duality of all things embraced by earlier cultures had been replaced by an overarching sense of dualism that sought to divide all things.

In the sixth or seventh century B.C., Zoroaster founded a Persian religion that featured two gods, one of light and good (Ormazd), and one of dark and evil (Ahriman). The task for Zoroastrians was to fix nature, rather than to live in harmony with it. The followers of this religion believed that a savior would eventually help eliminate all evil, so that there would be nothing but good and light. Rather than learning to live with both the bright and dark aspects of nature, these ancestors of western civilization began to lose their integration and relationship to earth. Subtly, the vital symbols and myths of these people changed, and they began to focus on the eradication of evil. These new beliefs left people irrevocably estranged from nature, and that separation from nature represented a significant vulnerability.[7]

Hopes and Fears

Injustices were common in these male-dominated cultures. According to Stone (1976), women were considered the property of either their husbands or their fathers. The prophets and priests systematically killed people who still believed in the religion of the goddess-oriented cultures. Stone believes these cultures had to be destroyed so that women could be persuaded to accept their position as their husbands' property. Stone notes that women were regarded as mindless and carnal creatures, and these types of attitudes were supposedly proven by the Paradise myth.

The creation myth of Adam and Eve symbolically blamed women for sexual consciousness. Stone (1976) believes that, from that time on, women were viewed as sexual temptresses. When the serpent gave the fruit to Eve and she urged Adam to eat it, the resulting catastrophe was blamed on Eve and the serpent. Therefore sex was considered immoral, sinful, and shameful. In the goddess-oriented myths that predated the Paradise myth, the serpent had been revered as a female symbol—the symbol of life—and it had been associated with prophecy and divine revelation. To eat the fruit of the Tree of Knowledge was to eat the flesh of the Goddess—to embrace life. Sexuality was part of a spiritual existence whereby one could practice love, compassion, and forgiveness in relationships and be reminded of one's interdependence and oneness with all. Regrettably, western culture is still heavily influenced by the myths that perceive sexuality in negative terms and emphasize male supremacy. For example, there are still double standards regarding premarital virginity; there are also high levels of rape and other violence toward women.[8]

Even deeper than the sexual fears reflected in the creation myth is the fear of the duality of all things. A dualistic approach seeks to resolve this fear by dividing the divine and the natural selves, pronouncing one good and the other evil. The Tree of Knowledge was also known as the Tree of Knowledge of Good and Evil—a symbol of passage from unity into the field of opposites. Once Adam and Eve had eaten the fruit, they saw distinctions where before they had seen only likenesses. They suddenly knew they were naked and different from one another and felt ashamed of their nakedness. Ironically, the gender that through the goddess myths had symbolized the unity inherent in duality was, in the creation myth, blamed for the dualism that brought about the fall from grace. One might see this also as a fall from our recognition of our oneness with the divine.

The Separation

Western philosophies and religions gradually became dominant. Many of their basic concepts are rooted in Greek philosophy. Prior to the Indo-European invasion, cultural traditions in Greece spoke of a primal state of unity—the womb of the great mother, from which all diversity emerged (Spretnak, 1991). However, this changed, as illustrated by the writings of Greek philosophers who posited a dualism of mind and body, of spirit and matter. With a patriarchal social structure in place, and nature increasingly displaced from its sacred status, human beings were considered separate from nature. The Greeks believed that the freedom of the soul could be gained only through rational thought. Although their contributions in terms of rational thought were enormous, their separation from nature prevented our ancestors from accepting both the horrors and the beauties of the world. Rather than being a part of nature, we declared ourselves fundamentally different from nature and took on the task of improving the world.

When we began to see ourselves as separate from nature, we began losing our sense of interconnection with the earth. In metaphorical terms, we were expelled from the Garden. As we increasingly attempt to dominate and control the forces of nature—rather than live in harmony with them—we alter the evolutionary balancing processes that constantly take place among the various life forms and fail to recognize the forces of nature acting within our own bodies. Overpopulation, the despoiling of the environment, and other environmental catastrophes are all consequences of this tendency to control rather than live with nature.

Although the belief in our dominion created a vulnerability, the effects of that vulnerability were for a time mitigated by other conditions in early societies. Most people still lived in small communities and were dependent upon nature and the land for their survival. Many incorporated parts of the goddess-oriented cultures into their new western religions. For example, in Christianity, the goddess figure came back in the form of the Virgin Mary (Campbell, 1980). The idea that we are essentially different from nature and can control it had no serious ecological consequences when resources were abundant and the world was sparsely populated.[9]

The Rise of Science

During the tenth, eleventh, and thirteenth centuries, in other parts of the world, civilizations flourished that were clearly more advanced than the warring feudal states of Europe. In 1295 Marco Polo returned from Kublai Kahn's China, bearing silk, porcelain, and tales of a spectacular civilization that held riches beyond anyone's imagination. In the next three hundred years, one of the most remarkable transformations in human history occurred, as Europe became the most important center of power in the world.[10] The period now called the Renaissance was a time of monumental change in Europe.[11]

New technologies emerged largely because of a new openness to ideas and scientific inquiry that flourished during that period. Through the new technologies and through systems of managing large states that emerged and were refined during the Renaissance, European leaders gained the tools and resources needed to conquer and dominate other continents. Thus a number of other cultures that had more reverent attitudes toward nature were colonized by the West.

In this new science, reason was valued and held sacred. Sir Francis Bacon became a propagandist for science, appealing for the use of experimentation to understand nature. Descartes believed that the world was ruled by mechanical forces, and that scientists' new instruments could be used to find the truth. Scientific societies began forming all over Europe, and science became the model for all intellectual activities. Science was evolving into the new orthodoxy, though critics like Pascal feared this worship of science, believing that the truth could be apprehended only by faith and the heart.

The process of turning away from nature continued. The universe was now believed to be filled with dead matter, and the goal of the sciences was to find methods to control nature. The technology that quickly developed served the new demands of commerce and industry. The western separation of mind and body was now complete.[12] The second vulnerability, our need to increasingly control and dominate the forces of nature rather than to live in respectful balance with them, was now established.

LOSS OF EXTERNAL SYMBOLS AND GUIDEPOSTS

Vital religious symbologies had provided a sense of meaning for centuries. The third vulnerability, the elimination of external moral and religious guideposts, has cast many people into a sea of doubt. They can no longer rely on the nurturing and validating rituals and images that once gave human lives a foundation of meaning.

Science has saved lives and vastly improved the quality of life for many. On the other hand, some scientific discoveries have eroded our sense of certainty and place within the universe.

In the sixteenth century, Copernicus made a discovery that was astonishing at the time: the universe does not revolve around the earth (Copernicus, 1543/1995). If that knowledge shook our moorings in the cosmos, subsequent discoveries have disturbed our equilibrium even further. We now know that there are billions of stars in the galaxy and billions of galaxies. The earth is about four billion years old; one day our star will burn out. And before the big bang took place, all matter in the universe occupied less than one-tenth of a millimeter.

Darwin's theory of evolution, published in 1859, was a critical scientific breakthrough. Other discoveries followed, and soon science was investigating the stories in the Old and New Testaments. Romer's (1988) research has suggested that the stories of Genesis were taken from more ancient Mesopotamian myths. Others have suggested that the stories of the Garden of Eden, and Noah's ark and the flood, were taken from earlier Sumerian myths, which predated the Bible by two thousand years. While many of these claims have been disputed, it is significant that over the past few hundred years many respected scholars have begun questioning western religious beliefs (see, for example, Romer, 1988).

These modern ideas—that we have evolved from chimpanzees, rather than from the inhabitants of the Garden of Eden; and that the Earth is not the center of the universe, but only one insignificant planet in an endless universe of billions of galaxies—were not widely known or accepted by the average person before the late 1800s. For most people the Bible was the primary text; they were not aware of the controversies concerning the content of the religious texts raised by scientific findings. Their families, crafts, religions, and communities were still vital and nourishing to their lives and sense of well-being.

With more widespread education, more people began questioning their religious beliefs. By the early 1900s, some of the best-educated elite were pronouncing that God was dead. The symbols and images that had once guided people through their lives began to be seen by some as antiquated and erroneous. The existentialists, among others, now saw a world in which religious metaphors had been stripped of their meaning: Only internally created values were considered authentic. Classical Greek myths were reinterpreted to suggest new attitudes about how people perceived their world. In the original myth of Sisyphus, according to Hazel Barnes (1985), Sisyphus betrayed the secret love of Zeus in return for a better water system for Cornith. His punishment was to repeatedly push a rock up a hill, only to see it fall. This was the justice meted out to mortals who had the audacity to betray the gods. Camus (1982) retranslated this myth for the twentieth century. In his new version, Sisyphus was viewed as making a personal revolt, an assertion of human meaning against the indifference of the universe. Sisyphus was a hero because he created his own values where none had been offered to him. In another Greek myth, Orestes killed his mother and her lover because he was ordered to do so by Apollo. Orestes was acquitted of murder because his action was in accordance with the will of Zeus: Human justice was superseded by eternal divine justice. However, in Sartre's (1947) play *The Flies*, after the murders Orestes defies Zeus and by doing so affirms the freedom of man. In the twentieth century, justice is considered primarily the concern of human beings in their relations with one another rather than the result of divine decree. Our need, according to Sartre (1947), is to preserve self-dignity.

Our disillusionment with religion has led to years of wandering in the wilderness.[13] Believers, agnostics, and atheists were all soon confronted with the fourth vulnerability: the loss of connection with the land, crafts, and communities.

SEPARATION FROM THE LAND

Edmond Wilson (Kellert & Wilson, 1993) has coined the term "biophilia" to indicate our biological need for and love of nature. The need to be in the presence of nature is a genetic and fundamental part of our being. Research has found, for example, that hospital patients who have windows facing natural settings heal more rapidly than those whose windows do not. Unfortunately, millions of people now spend their lives separate from the land, in stressful urban environments. Separation from the world of nature makes people feel less safe and less lovable; it contributes to feelings of detachment and to a society that feels less care and concern.

The importance of the connection with family, community, and the land has been demonstrated repeatedly. For example, in studies of life satisfaction, the four variables that people most often identify as important are family, home, community, and neighborhood (Lyon, 1989). These studies show a deep inner need for human connectedness, community spirit, and neighborliness; and that these qualities are increasingly found lacking in our society (McLaughlin & Davidson, 1985). A historical analysis illuminates the reasons for these drastic changes in human relationships.

Throughout history people have lived in communal dwellings. Within villages people helped one another out—not as charity, but because it was part of the natural course of human life. At times village life was circumscribed by narrowness and provincialism; however, positive feelings of mutual respect, working together for common ends, and neighborliness provided nurturance and meaning. These communities had Gemeinschaft qualities: The natural spontaneous, organic relations of the people grew out of mutual affection, customs, and traditions. In contrast, our modern societies are dominated by Gesellschaft qualities: They feature formal organizations, contracts, and legislation. Morgan (1942) believed that organized society could survive only as long as it was invigorated by the spirit of the Gemeinschaft community. In recent times, we have gained greater individual freedom, but the cost of that freedom has been social isolation. We need to ask why these powerful changes have occurred during the past two hundred years.

Industrialization and Urbanization

Scientific advances paved the way for the Industrial Revolution, which contributed to the breakdown in the fabric of community living. In the 1800s many people moved to the cities, thus eroding their connection to the land. The crowded industrial cities of the nineteenth century were very unsanitary. Initially there were no sewage systems, so the water was often unsafe. In 1840 the average age of death in Manchester, England was 17.

The Industrial Revolution occurred in eighteenth-century Europe because a variety of necessary conditions existed (Upshur, Terry, Holoka, Goff, & Lowry, 1991). For example, England had easy access to raw materials, an adequate labor supply, markets for large quantities of manufactured goods, and a surplus of capital. In addition, the Age of Reason had encouraged scientific inquiry and experimentation, and there were legal, political, and social policies that protected entrepreneurs.

Stein (1960) has traced the roles of urbanization, industrialization, and bureaucratization in the movement of American society toward the Gesellschaft end of the continuum. Industrialization has replaced a sense of coherence and satisfaction with one's craft with a new emphasis on getting ahead. In the 1940s and 1950s, society became dedicated to an ever-rising standard of living. This justified the industrial work role but slowly replaced the traditional sense of community. Career-driven men led barren lives. Children were loved for what they did, rather than who they were. There was little time for intimate moments with family and friends. In this new society, high levels of alienation and isolation were common, and the local community ceased to be a place that mattered. Life transitions began to be minimized, and their rituals were commercialized or performed perfunctorily by impersonal social agencies, schools, or religious officiaries.

In contrast, primitive community life protected the integrity of the individual's life cycle. Ruth Benedict, Paul Radin, Meyer Fortes, and E. R. Leach explored cultures in which everyday life was imaginatively transformed and saturated with meaning (Stein, 1960). In these cultures, life transitions were honored. The people celebrated birth and death and performed a progression of rituals to mark all stages in the life cycle, from infancy to old age. People's lives were built upon spiritual foundations and maintained in balance with nature. Their lives were a natural and interrelated aspect of the community.

The Evolution of Values

During the past 150 years, sociologists and anthropologists have noticed a change in values within our culture. Prior to the Industrial Revolution, people's roles in crafts and farming were well defined, and these jobs gave meaning to their lives. Since the Industrial Revolution, there has been a greater emphasis on the individual, and the prevalent values have become more materialistic and self-oriented. As more people have moved from the village to the city, long-term bonds with the land have been severed, and community traditions have weakened.

Even with all of these problems, the family could have provided a foundation upon which individuals could build a sense of balance and coherence. Unfortunately, urbanization, the loss of meaningful work, and detachment from nature and religion have weakened family norms and values. As the values that glorify competition and individual achievement have gained ascendancy, they have also become the values that many families teach their children—by word or example. As people's senses of meaning and spiritual connectedness have dwindled, the consequent rise in substance abuse has robbed many families of their ability to effectively impart consistently nurturing values to their children. In addition, many children are raised in poverty. These children are confused and frustrated by televised scenes of opulence, which makes it difficult for parents to teach them appropriate values.

The Values of Men and Women

Our society's emphasis on aggressive masculine values has had deleterious effects on gender perception and child development. Gilligan (1982) claims that the leading psychological theorists of this century have interpreted the values of men and women with an unfortunate bias. In general, male behavior has been accepted as the norm, and female behavior has been considered a deviation from the norm. For example, because Freud believed that the superego was determined by castration anxiety, he concluded that women could not have a clear-cut Oedipal resolution, leaving them with a compromised superego and a diminished sense of justice. In addition, in his stages of moral development, Kohlberg (1981) assigns more women than men to a low developmental level (stage 3) because women see morality in interpersonal terms, centered on obligations to the self, the family, and other people. When women engage in "male" activities, Kohlberg places them in higher levels where relationships are subordinated to rules or to universal principles of justice. Of course, it is difficult to imagine a rule or a principle of justice governing a situation in which no relationship is being affected, either directly or indirectly.

Concern for relationships, or for being a caregiver or a helpmate, has been interpreted as a weakness. In contrast, the masculine focus on achievement and great ideas has defined most men's standards of success and has helped them achieve desired identities at work. However, most men lack both intimate male friendships and nonsexual friendships with women (Levinson, 1978). Their emotionally constricted relationships have been subordinated to the pursuit of achievement. Because masculine values prevail in our society, those whose values are different may begin to question the normality of their feelings.

Gilligan (1982) traces some of the differences in male and female values to early childhood. Women are largely responsible for early childhood care, be they mothers, other female relatives, or paid caregivers. Girls are naturally taught to identify themselves as female; during their first three years, most girls are freely allowed to experience attachment to and identification with their female caregivers. According to Chodorow (1974), boys are taught to define themselves as opposites of their female caregivers. For boys, separation from the mother figure tends to begin earlier and to take on greater existential significance, because it is considered essential to their assumption of the male role. Depending on the boy's circumstances, the separation process can be fraught with fear and rage; it can prompt him to curtail or distort his love for his mother and to deny his empathic tie with other human beings in general. Girls often emerge from the separation process with a basis of empathy that boys have not been allowed to develop (Rubin, 1976). Male gender identity is more easily threatened by intimacy, whereas female gender identity is more easily threatened by separation.

These early differences are manifested when children play. Boys usually enjoy quarreling as much as the games themselves, whereas disputes among girls tend to end their games (Lever, 1976). Boys are learning organizational skills and independence to prepare them for the modern corporate world through such activities as the coordination of diverse groups of enemies and friends. Caring for feelings has little value in the marketplace and can even lead to professional problems at work. Two distinct moral ideologies are evident: one focusing on separation, identification, and achievement; and the other on attachment, relationship, and caring. Rather than seeing both ideologies as important and necessary to a whole and balanced system, our society has clearly elevated one at the expense of the other. Society has an abundance of frustrated power seekers. Individuals who continually strive for more personal authority at the expense of human connections tend to suffer more bouts of illness than do their less driven counterparts (McClelland, 1979). A historical perspective helps explicate the process by which the focus on achievement and individuation has become salient.

THE IMPORTANCE OF A HISTORICAL PERSPECTIVE

History helps us understand our present problems and their relationship to four complex, overlapping vulnerabilities. New myths have separated us from our mother earth, as society increasingly tries to control and dominate the forces of nature rather than to live in respectful balance with them. In the process, some valuable biological animal instincts have been rejected. Religious belief systems have increasingly been questioned and rejected. Rather than accepting the mysteries of life, many religions have concretized their mythology, as if its importance lay in specific historical events, rather than in metaphorical images and the timeless truths they represent. Once the mystery and vitality of these symbols were taken away, the inevitable consequence was an emotional wasteland (Campbell, 1969). Finally, our last refuge—our connection with crafts, the land, and the community—has slowly eroded, as people have moved away from small communities in search of employment in depersonalized cities. During the past few hundred years we have lost our special place in the universe, we have been displaced from the land, and we have been divorced from our small communities and families. Greed and desire have desecrated our mother earth and seriously wounded our psyches. Power struggles and a need for control have tipped the gentle balance within us. Acting as a conquering people, we have defeated ourselves.

Clearly, this bleak picture does not characterize all contemporary citizens of industrialized countries. Some individuals have accepted their genetic underpinnings and found a healthy balance with the forces of nature. They have incorporated into their lives religious or spiritual images that remain vital and nourishing and have found supportive and healing families and communities, even within urban areas. Western civilization has made many valuable contributions (Schlesinger, 1992). Western writers have proposed ideas that have had revolutionary positive impacts on the advancement of personal liberties and human rights and on freedom of inquiry and expression. Western advocates have abolished slavery and torture in their societies, improved the status of women, and combated racism. We can be proud of these legacies and many others like them. There are vital traditions within western civilization that can be used as antidotes to the four vulnerabilities described in this chapter.

Furthermore, many ancient cultures committed gross violations of basic human rights. They practiced slavery and discriminated against low-caste groups. They accepted the abuse of women and children and reserved education for the elite. Some people may argue that our current society is no worse than those of the past. However, in spite of their many unacceptable practices, ancient cultures were more often connected to the land, had stronger sustaining beliefs and values, and grew stronger and more enduring family and community roots. Although many of the past abuses, such as slavery, have been eliminated in the United States, the four vulnerabilities help explain some of the breakdowns in community that we are witnessing.

Problems and Solutions

Clearly, in our country as well as in many other western-oriented cultures, problems of urban decay, crime, homelessness, drug abuse, and environmental degradation run rampant. This book posits that these symptoms of the breakdown in our sense of community are connected to the vulnerabilities presented in this chapter. An analysis of these vulnerabilities will help us identify remedies for strengthening our culture and our society.

From a western perspective, a healthy individual should have sturdy foundations in four areas: the body, which should have strength and endurance; the mind, which should be adept at creativity, problem solving, and accruing knowledge; the spiritual domain, which should have goals and visions that help direct and focus life; and the social arena, which should have strong connection with family and friends. In this book I suggest that these four domains can be richly expanded upon by borrowing from other wisdom traditions. Using this broadened perspective, one might strive to inculcate the following features: a balanced and flexible energy field within the body, long posited by Eastern yogis as a source of health and well-being; a peaceful and quiet mind, advocated by meditators from a variety of religious traditions; a spiritual sense of interconnectedness and oneness, supported by those who live within a variety of mystical traditions; and a reverence for nature and others, a social domain advocated by a number of cultures, including that of Native Americans. It is to these broadened attributes of a well-balanced and healthy life that we turn in the following chapters.

3

A New Paradigm for Hope

Practice loving kindness to overcome anger. Loving kindness has the capacity to bring happiness to others without demanding anything in return. Practice compassion to overcome cruelty. Compassion has the capacity to remove the suffering of others without expecting anything in return. Practice sympathetic joy to overcome hatred. Sympathetic joy arises when one rejoices over the happiness of others and wishes others well-being and success. Practice non-attachment to overcome prejudice. Non-attachment is the way of looking at all things openly and equally. . . . Myself and other are not separate.

—Thich Nhat Hanh
Old Path White Clouds

FROM SHADOW TO VISION

More than 2,500 years ago, Plato wrote a story of mystery and discovery. In this metaphorical tale, people were living in a cave, and all they could see were shadows. The cave dwellers believed that this darkened version of reality was all that existed. One man left the cave, saw the world of colors and light, and came back to tell his people. Unfortunately, they didn't believe that what he had seen was possible, so they remained in the cave, with their safe but constricted experience of the world (Cornford, 1966). The story of Plato's cave is as meaningful today as it was in ancient Greece. We all wear lenses that prevent us from seeing new dimensions of the world. The fish swimming in a pond have little concept of the creatures viewing them from above. We also need to stretch our visions and our willingness to see new domains, if we are to rise above the vulnerabilities discussed in the previous chapter.

Bellah, Madsen, Sullivan, Swidler, and Tipton (1985) have observed our increasing emphasis on the individual and our tendency to look for fulfillment in the accumulation of income and status. They believe that social interventions are needed to help people recover the narrative unity of their lives. Families could be nurtured by drawing on the larger community. Our lives could become enriched by helping and supporting others and celebrating this life-sustaining and vitalizing process.

Bellah and his colleagues state that existing traditions can create a morally and intellectually intelligible world, and that these culturally rich traditions can be conveyed through our families, churches, and cultural associations. In religious texts such as the Old and New Testaments, societies sharply divided between rich and poor were seen as going against the wishes of God. Bellah and his colleagues ask whether we can find ways to share our material wealth with others and learn to make work intrinsically interesting and valuable. The enormous challenge before us is to find practices that are inherently fulfilling, such as worship in which we express our gratitude and wonder for the mystery of life and show love and friendship for our fellow citizens. In the sections that follow, I examine several disciplines to identify energizing ideas that might help in the creation of an alternative model of community, social, and psychological healing. The next section begins with an analysis of our educational system, a setting that has the potential to inculcate fresh ideas that are invigorating and nourishing.

EDUCATION: FROM CRISIS TO HOPE

Our educational systems are still guided by ideas from the Industrial Age, in which 85 percent of all workers were engaged in repetitive tasks and 15 percent were managers. In the new Information Age, all workers will need to be familiar with technology and problem solving. The microchip is in the process of amplifying human intelligence, just as the Industrial Revolution amplified the human muscle (Dobyne and Crawford-Mason, 1991). However, 10 to 30 percent of our population is illiterate. The crisis in our schools is selective, with many schools in affluent areas giving children excellent preparation for the Information Age that is to be their home, while schools in inner cities are close to collapse, with neither children nor teachers wanting to be there. By the year 2000, 42 percent of children attending public schools will be living in poverty (U.S. Bureau of the Census, 1986). The unequal distribution of resources, along with top-down bureaucratic systems that encourage obedience rather than creativity, create serious impediments to resolution of this crisis. Sarason (1972) maintains that the diversity and number of children, plus the perceived responsibility to cover a specified amount of material, make the task of real teaching impossible. Furthermore, when the experience of teaching is no longer exciting for teachers, the experience of learning cannot be interesting for children. Sarason and Klaber (1985) suggest that encapsulated schools are not the best settings for effective education.

Kohlberg, Ricks, and Snarey (1984) maintain that underachievement predicts all major forms of adult maladjustment, and that factors other than intelligence, such as learning, attention, and a sense of competence, that contribute to school achievement are established in the first three grades. Many of our educational interventions have focused on increasing a fixed level of school achievement; however, it may be more important to cultivate positive skills and attitudes about learning, coping, and ego development. Emotional intelligence, which includes awareness of emotions, emotional self-regulation, optimism, and empathy, may be a relevant, appropriate, and even essential goal of our educational institutions (Goldman, 1995).

The progressive education movement, inspired by John Dewey, focused on these types of innovative goals, with methods that include experiential learning, democratic classroom practices, and community-based learning. Schools such as the one developed by Dewey in 1896 at the University of Chicago were places of action, thought, and ideas, and teachers had the freedom to invent their own curricula (Sarason, 1972). Rather than a preparation for life, schools need to be an integral part of life.

Values in Education

Several contemporary authors have examined educational systems within our country, and they have concluded that new sets of values and actions are needed. One of the most important theorists in the educational arena is Paulo Freire. Freire believes that education is not neutral: It can be used either to domesticate or to liberate. For Freire, education must begin by first helping people identify the issues they have strong feelings about and then helping them search for solutions to their problems actively rather than passively. Everyone in the community needs to be involved in the transformation of a new society, and all can serve as both teachers and pupils (Hope & Timmel, 1985).

Borrowing from the work of Freire, Purpel (1989) concluded that schools represent powerful social, intellectual, and personal forces, which reflect the culture's consciousness. For many children and adolescents, the principal lessons learned are how to be obedient and passive, how to work on meaningless tasks without complaining, how to value achievement and competition, and how to please and respect authority figures. These lessons are inappropriate preparation for an increasingly interdependent world in which justice, compassion, and community should be the overriding considerations.

Purpel believes that a religious and moral framework would energize our schools and our culture by providing images that have force and meaning. A gift from our intellectual heritage, the Greek passion for freedom of inquiry and tolerance for different points of view, could represent the foundational element of an emerging myth. Socrates believed that education could be used to teach virtue and a critical examination of conventional thinking. The first step in a spiritual or educational journey involves an admission that one doesn't know and that one is open and flexible to many possibilities. A life worth living, as described in *The Republic of Plato* (Cornford, 1966), would be devoted to justice. In the early utopia Plato described, neither riches nor power could make an individual or a society happy. For Plato, knowledge could be attained only after a long and rigorous search, and this journey was made more complex by the limitation that the senses provide only an imperfect copy of reality. The highest reality was the good, and this concept was formally identified with God (Kitto, 1967). Knowledge of God was richer and wider than anything else, and this knowledge culminated the search for inner reality.

The modes of inquiry developed by Socrates and Plato can be used to judge the moral adequacy of a culture (Purpel, 1989). In addition, our moral heritage could borrow from the prophetic traditions, which protested oppression, poverty, and inequality. Different religious traditions were used by Mahatma Gandhi and Martin Luther King, Jr., in their struggles for justice and equality. Gandhi used nonviolent resistance to liberate India. He found the core theme of nonviolence in the Bhagavad-Gita, which clearly advocates war. Gandhi believed that the stories of war in the Bhagavad-Gita were allegories and that the people of each age must retranslate them in light of their times and their spiritual knowledge (McCann, 1991). King also developed non-violent strategies to defeat segregation laws that were widespread in the United States. Two of the prominent attitudes of this nonviolence tradition are gratitude and contrition. Finally, we can borrow from our own political heritage, which features democratic principles. Government that requires the consent of the governed can affirm the dignity and autonomy of the individual.

Students and non-students alike can draw from these traditional orientations to enhance justice and cultivate a sense of joy and appreciation for the awe and mystery of the world. Purpel suggests that education should begin with the concerns that stir us to seek answers. Important questions might include What do we hold to be sacred? What are we willing to commit ourselves to? Who are we? How do we acquire knowledge and find meaning? The key issue is our quest to create a culture of abundance, joy, freedom, and justice.

Watts and Abdul-Adil (1994) outlined five stages of sociopolitical development, stages that could be employed in helping people become more actively involved in social change. In the acritical stage, people feel powerless and inferior and believe that those with low status deserve it. In the adaptive, pre-critical, and critical stages, people gradually learn more about the social and historical roots of injustice and oppression. Finally, in the liberation stage, people become involved in social action and community development.

These stages of change could be introduced into the curricula of many schools, and students could actually participate in bringing about changes in their schools and their communities. As an example of how these ideas can be translated into action, I myself developed an undergraduate course in which each student developed and launched a community-based intervention. Examples of projects the students worked on included setting up no-smoking sections in the cafeteria, developing procedures to ensure that only drivers with disabilities used the handicapped parking facilities, decreasing litter at community settings, ensuring that lights were not left on in unoccupied rooms, helping get a stop sign erected at a dangerous school intersection, and increasing the number of sidewalks shoveled after snowstorms (Jason, 1984).

Some schools have competent leadership, and teachers are given the authority to be creative and independent. When the right combination occurs, its chemistry produces a respect for differences, a regard for achievement, and a nurturing of the process of becoming an explorer of learning. When teachers take joy in their work, when schools take pride in their mission, the chances of producing important, sustainable changes are enhanced.

Values in Action: An Inner-City Success Story

Many teachers and parents are concerned about the increasing number of children who transfer from school to school each year (Jason et al., 1992). Some school transferees were doing poorly in their prior schools; transfers represent the parents' hope that new settings will be better for their vulnerable children. Other transferees were coping well in their prior schools, but experienced problems following their transfers. A transfer is a marker event, and some children experience symptoms or exacerbated problems as a result of the transition.

What can be done for such children from a social competence-oriented approach? Children with academic and social deficits will need remedial interventions, and if these interventions are implemented soon enough, the potential for prevention of further problems is great. An ecologically sensitive approach may be more promising, however. Let me be more specific. I recently had an inspiring conversation with the principal of an inner-city school and found that her school successfully uses the students' own cultural values to retain and sustain students. Although wages are low, the vast majority of teachers return year after year. In the student population, the transfer rate out of the school is exceedingly low. On Fridays all children who have not been in trouble during the week are given a special assembly or event. The school policy is to avoid expelling children. The principal plays the role of cheerleader, wandering through the halls and providing support and encouragement to teachers and children alike. If a teacher or child is experiencing problems, extra help is provided.

I was impressed with the results of this ecologically sensitive approach to education. Would these types of organizational values affect a school's individual-centered social competence interventions? Of course! If a school views its mission as that of giving vulnerable children the information, experiences, and support they need to be successful, then it will undoubtedly achieve higher academic ratings.

The principal said that her own values were consistent with those of the cultures represented by the school's children, increasing her ability to support their traditions, mores, and customs. She identified one of the primary reasons schools fail—leadership roles are occupied by individuals who neither understand nor appreciate the skills, interests, and special needs of inner-city children of color. Can we really be expected to succeed when we are devaluing, and thus eroding, the very strengths of those we are mandated to repair?

Myths and Rituals Restored

What myths and expectations are being conveyed to us and our children, powerfully influencing our work as professionals and our children's reactions to that work? In more primitive times, rituals, customs, and rites helped ease the transition from the dependent status of youth to the independence of adulthood. Some of the problems within our youth probably represent misguided attempts to deal with the loss of myths and rituals that gave precious generations more tangible senses of meaning in society. Social problem-solving strategies could be used to explore the remnants of myths and rituals that still reside within our youth and to actively help them recreate a mythology that is meaningful to their families and communities.

An innovative educational program called ROPE (Rite of Passage Experience) provides rituals of initiation for adolescents (Blumenkrantz & Gavazze, 1993). Over a six-year period, children undergo symbolic experiences that help them learn to navigate their life experiences. In addition to exploring different cultures' rites of passage, children are provided group team-building experiences, such as rope courses, rock climbing, and community service, in which having fun is validated as an important part of growing up. Children who participate in this program have significantly fewer delinquent activities and lower drug and alcohol consumption than children who do not participate.

Another innovative program is The Mysteries, developed by Shelley Kessler at a private school for seventh- to twelfth-grade students in Santa Monica, California. The goal of The Mysteries is to give teenagers a larger social and spiritual framework and a sense of meaning as they make the transition to adulthood. At an initial orientation session, students are seated in a circle and an Indian "talking stick" is passed from child to child. Only the person holding the stick can talk. Other activities include meditation, guided imagery, a wide variety of games, and a five-day wilderness retreat during the senior year. Children have opportunities to clarify their values and goals, learn to listen and respond sincerely rather than to judge, develop their intuition and imagination, acquire an understanding and tolerance of human diversity, and develop a sense of responsibility for the environment.

The Mysteries teaches ideals from the world's great spiritual traditions. Unfortunately, many academics reject metaphysical themes because of the negative images associated with them. However, it would be a mistake to ignore the great insights and wisdom traditions that have been handed down from all cultures and all ages. Our children are very much in need of serenity in thought and cessation of the anguish of the mind (Buddhism), appreciation of the earth body and the human body (the goddess religions), reverence for nature (Native Americans), love for others (Gnosticism), a sturdy social ethic (the three great western religions), and joy and play as they participate in the mystery of life (Hinduism). Reclaiming these meaningful traditions would help us return to a balance with nature that would restore the sense of connectedness with life that people once had with their communities and their land.

The real task is to help each person find his or her personal mythology. People will have to search their own experiences and cultures and other traditions for the symbols and rituals that energize and vitalize them. Simply imitating picturesque rituals that seem to have deep meaning for others will not be enough, however. Individuals will have to blend the old and the new, the foreign and the familiar; they will have to focus on the meaning beneath the stories and symbols. If we use care and intelligence in encouraging and facilitating this exploration, the process will be lifted above the empty ritual practiced in some traditional celebrations and the blind faddishness associated with some contemporary New-Age practices.

PHILOSOPHICAL VIEWS OF FOUNDATIONAL VALUES

Philosophical systems, or world views, often have pervasive shaping influences on the subjects scientists choose to study. These models help focus scientists' attention on certain problems and ideas but always at the exclusion of other problems and ideas. During the past four hundred years, the sciences have been wedded to the paradigm of logical positivism. This paradigm emphasizes control and determinism; it has allowed scientists to study natural phenomena in simple and controlled settings. The logical positivism paradigm assumes the possibility of certain knowledge; its proponents often search for foundational information. Practitioners of this approach deride metaphysics and subjectivity. Logical positivism has been used profitably by most professionals in the hard sciences, such as physics; but its vision of a mechanical universe has been viewed suspiciously by many in the social sciences.

Community psychologists and others involved in analyzing social and community change posit a different epistemological paradigm. Contextualism, a primary feature of this alternative paradigm, has been defined by Kingry-Westergaard and Kelly (1990) as our embeddedness in the world we observe. In contextualism, knowledge is relevant only within a given frame of reference. This idea was further developed by Bry, Hirsch, Newbrough, Reischl, and Swindle (1990), who view knowledge as limited by its historical and cultural context. They believe that we do not simply glean knowledge from our objective observations of an objective world but that the nature of the knower contributes to the nature of what is known, implying that science tells us as much about the investigator as it does about the phenomena being studied. A final component of contextualism is an epistemology currently espoused by many feminists, among others, recommending that we empower people by listening to them and understanding them from their points of view. When people are studied in research projects, they should be treated not as subjects but as participants. These ideas hint at a paradigm that disavows the possibility of foundational knowledge. For that reason, the contextualist paradigm may hold some hidden dangers. Taken to its extreme, it can lead to the loss of all connection with foundational values, a loss exemplified in the contemporary philosophy called deconstructive postmodernism.

Deconstructive postmodernism, which is based on the work of Jacques Derrida, has its roots in the objective era. During that era, as indicated in the previous chapter, God was replaced by science. In the early years of the twentieth century, the existentialists took this notion one step further, concluding that the universe was meaningless and indifferent. In his philosophy, the sense of separation from nature was complete. Many in today's artistic and intellectual circles have embraced the philosophy of deconstructive postmodernism. This world view posits that there are no universal truths, but rather that all concepts are culturally constructed and all meaning is temporary and relative. Adherents believe that this philosophy will liberate its proponents from all domination, but its critics fear that this liberation could lead to valuelessness. Spretnak (1991) suggests that this fashionable philosophy leads to a sense of groundlessness, detachment, and shallow engagement.

During the past hundred years, eastern thought and philosophies from native peoples have contributed to an alternative way of seeing the world. Leading proponents of this model included German romantic philosophers such as Schelling, American transcendentalists such as Emerson and Thoreau, English romantic poets such as Blake, and the Theosophical Society, which began in England. In contrast to logical positivism, contextualism, and deconstructive postmodernism, this model—ecological postmodernism—provides for a more vibrant sense of interconnectedness, one that is conscious of the unity in which we are all embedded (Spretnak, 1991). Unlike the supporters of deconstructive postmodernism, proponents of ecological postmodernism believe in the possibility of foundational values. Through wisdom traditions in a variety of cultures and religions, one can better understand the truths of being, "the flux, dynamism, subjectivity, creativity, and inherent relatedness" (Spretnak, 1991; p. 24).

For Spretnak, foundational values can be found in Buddhist efforts to bring serenity to the mind; in Native Americans' reverence for and balance with nature; and in religions that practice communion with and love for one's spouse, one's children or one's God.[14]

PHYSICS: TOWARD PERCEPTION OF ONENESS

In *The Structure of Scientific Revolutions*, Thomas Kuhn (1962) challenged the thesis that science was synonymous with the truth. Scientists work within a paradigm, defined in the scientific context as a set of rules and standards for solving scientific problems. When a new paradigm emerges, it gives scientists a new set of tools that helps them answer a new set of questions. In the physical sciences, Copernicus, Newton, and Einstein produced scientific revolutions by introducing new paradigms, which provided new problems worthy of being studied and new technologies for studying them. Scientists adopt new paradigms to understand nature more completely; however, these new models are mere lenses, through which they can only see the secrets of nature more clearly. The world of science cannot provide fundamental truths, only glimpses or hints of the intricacies of our complex world.

Most scientists have been aligned with the paradigm of logical positivism. From the perspective of Newtonian physics, the universe was a huge mechanical system. Solid objects were composed of atoms, and all things were subject to objective description. This reductionist orientation treats each system as mechanical, with its parts isolated from those of other systems. This paradigm has given rise to a technology that has dominated the world and is leading us toward ecological disaster (Briggs & Peat, 1989).

The new science of chaos is based on wholeness and interrelationships, and the unpredictability of nature (Briggs and Peat, 1989). The field of chaos theory is part of a larger field of mathematics called nonlinear dynamics. Most natural systems are seemingly unpredictable; however, chaos theory allows scientists at times to perceive simple patterns at higher levels of abstraction (Taubes, 1990). For example, in the early 1960s Lorenz was simulating weather conditions using nonlinear equations, and he found that entirely different weather patterns occurred when the initial conditions, such as air movement, differed in increments as small as those caused by the fluctuation of a butterfly's wings (the butterfly effect). Rather than focusing on traditional concerns such as prediction, control, and analysis of parts, the study of chaos concentrates on an awareness of the oneness of all things and on the unpredictability of the whole of things (Lorenz, 1967).

The macroscopic illusion of solidity began to disappear when scientists delved into the subatomic world and found that the protons and neutrons that comprise atoms are composed primarily of empty space, with minute particles (frozen packages of light) rapidly traversing this void. In essence, everything is made up of three types of particles: quarks, leptons, and gluons, which hold the other two together. Inside the protons and neutrons, quarks travel at more than 60,000 miles per second (Taubes, 1990).

At a microcosmic level, all matter is composed of highly organized energy fields (Gerber, 1988). With Einstein's discovery of relativity, scientists came to understand that matter can be converted to energy and vice versa. Fluctuations of energy cause particles to decay into other particle forms and then to resume their earlier forms. In a sense, our universe is filled with particles that are constantly coming into and out of existence. Matter does not exist with certainty in fixed places but only shows a tendency to exist in certain places.

Bell's theorem suggests that subatomic particles are connected in some way that transcends space and time. All is interconnected, and anything affecting one particle affects other particles. As Briggs and Peat state (1989):

> The universe must be fundamentally indivisible, a "flowing wholeness," as Bohm calls it. . . . Parts seem autonomous, [but] they are only relatively autonomous. They are like a music lover's favorite passage in a Beethoven

> symphony . . . the passage is meaningless without the symphony as a whole. . . . Bohm's ideas give a scientific shape to the ancient belief that "the universe is one." (p. 21)

Even one of the oldest sciences is inexorably moving toward a new paradigm for understanding the world.

PSYCHONEUROIMMUNOLOGY: CHARTING THE MIND–BODY CONNECTION

A relatively new field called psychoneuroimmunology has embraced some of the new ideas of ecological postmodernism (Jason, 1993). Psychoneuroimmunologists posit that the nervous, endocrine, and immune systems are in constant communication with one another (Kiecolt-Glaser & Glaser, 1989). In the early part of this century, the effects of negative thoughts, emotions, and expectations on health and behavior were convincingly documented; for example, voodoo spells have caused the deaths of numerous people who believed that the spells were real (Cannon, 1935). In the mid-1970s, Ader and Cohen's pioneering work (1975) indicated that the immune system can be conditioned, suggesting that our thoughts and surroundings can cue immune enhancement or suppression. Cousins (1989) believed that everything influenced the immune system: "The immune system is a mirror of life, responding to its joy and anguish, its exuberance and boredom, its laughter and tears, its excitement and depression, its problems and prospects" (35). Candace Pert (1986) has found receptors for tiny proteins, called peptides, throughout the body, and she believes it is through these peptides that feelings and emotions from the mind are transmitted into the physical realm, causing health or disease. Kiecolt-Glaser, Garner, Speicher, Penn, and Glaser (1984) found that, under negative emotional conditions (stress, depression, loss of control, learned helplessness, high anxiety, bereavement, loneliness, and extremely inhibited power motivation), disease fighting immune cells are depleted (Locke & Colligan, 1987). In contrast, support and relaxation training strengthen the immune system.[15]

The Role of Thought and Affect in Healing

Cohen and Williamson (1991) have reviewed many studies that found a relationship between stress and increased illness. For example, infectious diseases caused by common germs such as streptococcus bacteria have been related to both acute and chronic stress (Meyer & Haggarty, 1962). Kasl, Evans, and Niederman (1979) studied mononucleosis infection among cadets who were not immune to the disease. Those who contracted mononucleosis were very committed to a military career, performed poorly academically, and had fathers who were described as overachievers. This study suggests that there may be many factors—including stress, susceptibility, and coping styles—that make people candidates for infectious diseases. Kobasa, Maddi, Puccetti, and Zola (1985) found that individuals who were hardy (felt meaning in their lives, had a sense of mastery over life circumstances, and viewed problems as challenges), exercised, and obtained social support had an 8 percent likelihood of illness, whereas individuals without these qualities had a 92 percent likelihood of illness. Recent evidence suggests that social support, stressful events, and coping style influence immune function; however, some investigators believe we need to temper our enthusiasm for this new field because there is no definitive evidence linking psychological states to specific immune diseases (Bower, 1991).

Strategies pioneered in the emerging field of psychoneuroimmunology could possibly be employed to enhance functioning in people who are vulnerable to disease. Relaxation training and meditation can reduce despair and depression and enhance commitment, faith, hope, and joy (Kabat-Zinn, 1991; Locke & Colligan, 1987). These strategies may be particularly useful for helping people become more resilient to stressors and disease.

Finding hope and improving mood are important tasks for normal individuals who may be susceptible to stress-related disorders, as well as for those afflicted with a variety of other disorders. The prevention strategies used in psychoneuroimmunology may protect people from the ravages of a flood of immune-depressing biochemicals. Positive emotions may even enhance the recovery of formerly impaired immune functions. For some, a new sense of hope and optimism is enough to allow their bodies to heal. These individuals can begin enjoying life, and as new energy is mobilized, they are able to continue to believe in their treatment or prevention plans. Psychoneuroimmunology provides a theoretical reference point for understanding the powerful influence of the mind on prevention, behavior change, and healing processes.

Alternative Medicine: Healing the Effects of Alienation

In *Quantum Healing: Exploring the Frontiers of Mind/Body Medicine*, Deepak Chopra describes a new paradigm for understanding the healing process. In traditional western medicine, according to Chopra, "magic bullets," such as sleeping pills for insomnia and tranquilizers for anxiety, are prescribed to solve problems of living. However, in *Quantum Healing*, which emphasizes relationships between the mind and body, an effort is made to address a person's alienation from other people and from his or her environment. Since 1984 Chopra has been bringing together the best of ancient wisdom and modern science in an effort to help people make better use of their bodies' own pharmacies and capacities for self-healing. Chopra (1994) has also proposed seven "spiritual laws" of successful living; these laws have powerful implications for healing. Chopra believes that we need to learn to connect more effectively with the spirit, by meditating, by communing with nature, or by being less judgmental. We need to give to others in a considerate and joyful way, imitating the flow of the abundant energy of the universe. Chopra believes that an abundance of choices are available to us at any moment, but that correct choices give us joy and fulfillment. If one is unaware of and therefore controlled by these choices, the universe is deterministic; but if one is aware and chooses actions that give satisfaction to oneself and others, then there is freedom in the world. The law of least effort suggests that one can accomplish more with bliss and harmony by doing less; the key is to harness the energy of the universe, which functions with little effort in a joyful and loving way. The law of detachment suggests that we stop being so completely associated with the roles we play. We need to be process oriented and walk with joy down the path of life, even if we never reach our particular goals. Finally, the law of purpose indicates that each of us has a unique, special talent to give to others; when we are using this talent, we feel timelessness, joy, and ecstasy. According to Chopra, the positive feelings associated with respect for natural laws are not mere ends in themselves; they can also enhance immune functioning and improve overall mental and physical health.

The New Medicine: Obstacles and Opportunities

Unfortunately, present-day Western medicine is dramatically decreasing physician-patient contact, with the result that physicians are too rushed to inquire as to the real concerns of patients (Goleman & Gurin, 1993). The medicine of the future will need to deal with these structural impediments to good patient care by providing high-quality time for full discussion of symptoms and treatment plans.

Dreher (1995) has summarized some of the most promising areas in the burgeoning field of mind-body medicine. Studies indicate that, by tuning into mind-body signals of discomfort, pain, and fatigue, acknowledging these to themselves and others, and asserting their own needs, people can enhance their psychological and physical well-being. Other attributes that optimize physical and mental health include hardiness (a sense of commitment, control, and challenge) and the development of many facets of one's personality. People who form relationships based on unconditional love and trust and are committed to helping others also tend to be healthier. The best of mainstream and alternative medicine is combined in the pioneering work of Dean Ornish (1991), who used meditation, yoga, and low cholesterol diets to reverse the effects of heart disease in advanced cardiac patients. Another research-practitioner in the alternative medicine arena is Herbert Benson (Benson & Stuart, 1992), a Harvard cardiologist who has shown that meditation can be used successfully to treat a wide variety of conditions, such as migraine headaches, chronic pain, and diabetes. In addition, David Spiegel (1991) has shown that women with phase-IV breast cancer who participate in support groups live significantly longer than those who don't receive this form of social support.

Mainstream medicine has developed sophisticated and effective technologies for treating many life-threatening illnesses. However, the majority of patients are treated by physicians not for these illnesses, but for more time-limited conditions, such as colds or influenza, or for conditions in which psychological problems play a prominent role in the symptoms. One key to healing these prevalent illnesses is to make patients feel connected, supported, and loved (Borysenko, 1993). Loving people do become ill, and it would be inaccurate to conclude that all illnesses have psychological causes or contributors. However, although we rarely know why people become ill, patients can use their health crises as opportunities to heal. The new approaches to healing will focus on enhancing optimism, peace of mind, and forgiveness; and on helping people reduce judgmentalism and criticism. The ultimate gift that some devastating health crises leave us is the ability to see all life as meaningful and sacred. For example, those who have near-death experiences often report seeing all things as interconnected and part of the whole. A psychoneuroimmunology model would endorse a holistic approach to wellness that involves the body, mind, and spirit. Meditation, journaling, ritual, imagery, nutrition, and prayer represent some of the most promising alternative approaches to wellness (Novick, 1995).

MYTHOLOGY AND HEALING

Myths help map our routes toward a deeper life, to the realm of amplified possibilities (Jean Houston, 1992). Adolescents need initiation rituals and rites of passage—a journey where the child dies and the adult emerges. Cultures once provided people with symbologies that refreshed the spiritual dimension. Social life brought people into accord with the world of nature. Today many people are seeking to find and articulate the myths that they live by—the powers within themselves that are asking for fulfillment and realization. Each person must create personal answers to the metaphoric themes of what he or she might be. The popularity of two novels with themes of spiritual exploration, James Redfield's (1994) *The Celestine Prophecy* and Marlo Morgan's (1994) *Mutant Message Down Under*, suggests in the American public a new interest and openness to mythic journeys.

The lack of mythologies to guide children through transitions has negative consequences for our youth. For example, after girls reach puberty, many begin to lose their voices of confidence and autonomy, prefer the anonymity of fitting in, and become depressed and bulimic (Gilligan, 1982). Those who do not lose their confidence and voices during this transition have been given nurturance, encouragement for their assertiveness, and protective cultural narratives and guideposts by their families and teachers. Life-affirming celebrations and ceremonies need to validate the changing biological and psychological processes in our adolescents. Currently, such transitions are marked by isolation, shame, guilt, and lack of communication.

Purposes and Functions of Mythology

There are many different ways of studying myths: the functional theory of Bronislaw Malinowski, the structural interpretations of Claude Levi-Strauss, the phenomenological theory of Mircea Eliade, and the psychoanalytic theory of Jung (Livingston, 1989). Jung believed that there were three layers of the psyche: the conscious mind, the personal unconscious (where repressed and forgotten parts of personal history reside), and the collective unconscious (the deepest level, where forms or images from different cultures and historical periods are stored). Within the collective unconscious are archetypes, for example, a hero who is able to overcome dragons and monsters. These hero images appear in each generation, and they allow ordinary people to free themselves from their misery and raise themselves to almost superhuman status and a more complete fulfillment of their potential (Livingston, 1989). Reflecting Jungian theory, Campbell (1969) believed that myths are the way the unconscious communicates with the conscious self to deal with some of the basic issues of life. The discussion below will borrow heavily on the work of Joseph Campbell; although he has been accused of not being a scholar and of oversimplifying mythology (Doniger, 1992), his ideas are intriguing.

According to Campbell, some myths render the reality of the horror of life—that we consume and are eventually consumed—as acceptable. For example, myths of many of the eastern religions and Native American cultures affirm that we consume others in order to live and tell ourselves elaborate stories to explain and ultimately make peace with this reality. Some cultures, such as the Janists in India and the Hinayana Buddhists, withdraw from this horror, and their mythology supports that withdrawal. Finally, some mythological systems, such as those embraced by the western religions, attempt to correct this horror by eradicating evil and improving the world.

Myths serve four functions (Campbell, 1969). The first function is cosmological, helping people draw conclusions about the beginnings of their world. The Garden of Eden creation story is an example of a cosmological myth. The second function is sociological, validating and supporting the social order. Examples of myths with sociological functions include those in which people are punished severely for breaking the caste system in India. The third function is psychological, occurring when myths help carry an individual through the crises of life, from infancy to old age. Myths depicting rites that help adolescents move from a dependency status to an independent role are examples of this function. These myths also help individuals integrate the darker sides of their lives. Finally, metaphysical myths deal with the "second half" of life. These myths deal with awakening a mystical sense of awe toward the universe or God.

The Journey of Growth and Healing

Joseph Campbell's book *The Hero with a Thousand Faces* provides an interesting look at the field of experience for which the hero's mythological journey serves as an eloquent metaphor. The inner journey begins with a recognition that something is wrong with the nature of the world or with the inner self. This felt incongruity or tension is a call to adventure, in which each person must travel a route where no one has journeyed before. The purpose of the trip is to find what is missing—that deepest sense of harmony, the mystery that captures our imagination and holds it so that time passes without our noticing it. A prototypical myth can be found in the Sir Galahad stories, among the myths of the knights in King Arthur's Court. These knights saw a group of angels carrying the Holy Grail covered by a cloth and decided to embark on a quest to find the Grail. They considered it a disgrace to set forth as a group, so each entered the forest where it was darkest, where there was no visible path, and where there was no one to lead the way. In other words, the quest, as depicted in western myths and literature, is an individual journey. One often encounters dangers on this mythical trip—and the dragons that one encounters are parts of oneself that one needs to incorporate. If this mythical trip succeeds, the travelers begin to divest themselves of their social roles to follow their own individual paths.

Some individuals might choose to follow a guru to find the Holy Grail; but in relinquishing one's independence, one might embark on a journey whose myths explore regions that are not relevant to one's heart. In the West, because there is more attachment to the ego and individualism is highly valued, it may be more difficult to follow the path of another. Campbell suggests that people from an eastern background, with enduring traditions of duty and obedience, might find a path involving obedience to a guru more compatible with their beliefs.

At the beginning stage of the mythical journey, the need is to develop oneself and slowly become initiated into the adult world. Mythologies once provided the rites that carefully equipped and nurtured adolescents for entry into the adult world. Without traditions, myths, and other guideposts, the process of constructing the self, and integrating its shadows into our conscious lives, is substantially more difficult. The shadows that need to be confronted are those aspects of our existence that have been repressed.

Childhood and the Shadow

From Freud (1901) to Bradshaw (1990), scholars have shown in meticulous detail how children's developmental experiences can be marred by parents' unrealistic expectations, abuse, and neglect. Horney (1970) has shown us the consequences of the absence or inconsistency of love, affection, and reliable care in childhood. Extreme dependence, hostility, and loneliness can be the result of early failure to learn how to move toward people by showing trust and friendliness, to move against people by standing up for one's rights, and to move away from people by enjoying privacy. Adler (1951) has shown how early feelings of inferiority can predispose one to later strivings to reach unrealistic goals. Heinz Kohut's self-psychology is one of the newer psychoanalytic conceptual frameworks for understanding a fragmented sense of self due to early trauma. According to Kohut, caregivers need to appreciate and respond with pleasure to a child's special qualities and initiatives (Lerner & Ehrlich, 1994). The child also needs to be able to look up to the caregiver as an image of calm and omnipotence. The adult who was given a sense of stability and self-confidence as a child can maintain a sense of self-confidence and positive feelings despite life's frustrations and disappointments. Failure in parental empathy can lead to an inadequate sense of self, one that is fragmented and discontinuous; as adults, people with low self-image tend to urgently seek affirmation from others or constantly search for people to admire.

These early experiences can cause emotional trauma, and their effects can last through adulthood and continually sabotage the adult's efforts to mend. The individual's mythical journey then includes seeing these wounds and learning to interpret past events in ways that preserve honor and integrity. Many studies in the field of behavioral medicine have indicated that repression of painful memories and emotions is linked to a number of physical diseases (Schwartz, 1990) and that speaking about upsetting experiences and their associated emotions can lead to positive health outcomes (Pennebaker, 1990). Those who successfully confront this part of their shadow selves can learn to live with the memories that no longer drain their vital energies. At the highest level, one learns to love oneself for doing the best one could have done during those early years.

The Mask

The next domain of the shadow is the existential dilemma of living a life in which our social and biological needs are met, but in which our persona—the mask that we wear—draws farther and farther away from our souls. Society often requires that we wear a mask of respect and order, but severe problems can occur if the ego identifies completely with the mask (Jung, 1956). As Laing (1967) has suggested, this divided self produces a vulnerability that can have devastating consequences for social adjustment. Many people dislike their jobs and social roles and have lifestyles that profoundly deplete the vital energies of their souls, yet they maintain their masks because they fear an unknown future. Taking off the mask marks the departure on a mysterious and frightening personal journey. It takes enormous courage and faith to begin a journey toward authenticity, on which one can reap the benefits of learning to follow one's own inner truth, as opposed to what society dictates.

The Balance of Opposites

Travellers on the mythical journey may confront other shadows created by imbalance and the debilitating consequences of excess (Jung, 1956). Extraverts are drawn to power; they are active in the outer world to prove themselves (in this concept Jung borrows heavily from the ideas of Adler). Introverts, on the other hand, are open to the impact of experiences, and they intimately feel warmth and love for the world (these dimensions were best captured in the writings of Freud). These two aspects of the personality are in everyone, and our need is to learn to balance the power and erotic drives. If one domain dominates the other, problems can occur. Jung believed that people have superior and inferior functions for receiving and evaluating experiences: intellect and feeling, sensing and intuiting, acting and accomplishing, and forming relationships and loving. The fully functioning person, according to Jung, can think, feel, sense, and intuit. Even if a person loves his or her work and has made peace with early childhood trauma or neglect, excesses in any of these functions can create vulnerabilities that can weaken the constitutional energies of the psyche over time. The mythical journey can bring people into contact with the dimensions of their personalities that have been underdeveloped or neglected, thus helping them increase their self-complexity. Self-complexity is the result of a process whereby one develops multiple selves as well as a central self that can organize and tolerate multiple versions of the self. Research by Linville (1987) supports the notion that people high in self-complexity are more resilient and less prone to depression and physical symptoms of illness.

Achieving a balance between contrasting styles has been the theme of several of the great philosophers and writers of the last century. Nietzsche (1964), for example, described the superman as someone who could incorporate two dimensions: the ability to think and the ability to feel and love. Similarly, Thomas Mann (1995) described erotic irony as the ability to simultaneously synthesize and transcend love and criticism. Mann defined love as compassion and affection toward the world, evidenced by insights such as the recognition that people are lovable for their faults. He defined criticism as the work of a piercing and keen mind that can detect faults.

Jung (1956) says that each of us has masculine and feminine qualities. In metaphorical terms, if both domains are honored and appreciated, one can better endure both the blaze of the sun and the tides of the moon. Campbell (1971) believes this is the underlying message of Homer's Odysseus, the first great epic of western literature. Because Odysseus had not learned to assimilate his female aspects, the gods sent him on a perilous journey in an attempt to complete him and to change his one-sided relationship with women. The story begins after his victory at Troy. As Odysseus was returning home, he and his men stopped at a town where they raped the women and plundered and robbed the citizens of their possessions. The gods disapproved of this behavior and summoned winds to blow him to the beginning of his soul journey. In his trip to the underworld, Odysseus first had to divest himself of his prior beliefs and lifestyle. In his interactions with Circe, a seductress who had the power to turn men to swine, Odysseus learned that he could not overwhelm her, and his aggression turned to *eros*—feelings of sexual and romantic passion. On the isle of Calypso, Odysseus lived with a nymph in a mature relationship. On his travels within the underworld—or the unconscious—Odysseus gradually learned that women could not be treated as pieces of property. To survive and complete the journey, he was compelled to incorporate aspects of himself that he had previously rejected. With his new insights, he was ready to come back into the real world and return to his wife Penelope. Through his journey, Odysseus developed a more mature and healthy relationship with women.

By integrating the opposite poles of one's nature and accepting the paradoxes inherent in human existence, one can begin to embrace and love the shadow. In many myths, the hero meets a dark force—usually a black knight, a dragon, or a whale—representing the rejected aspect of the self. The hero's task is to integrate the opposite aspects of the self. In mythology, these elementary ideas come up over and over in different cultures; Jung referred to these ideas and the characters who exemplify them as archetypes. In a given culture these folk ideas might appear specific to that culture, but the underlying messages are universal. Myths can move people by speaking to their souls.

Metaphysical Journeys

Psychological myths resolve around the development of the self, the recovery from childhood abuse or neglect, the development of an authentic self, and the integration of complementary aspects of the personality. Once these stages have been successfully achieved during the first part of life—however long it takes to complete that part—a different set of myths becomes more salient. During the second part of life, metaphysical journeys may begin (Campbell, 1969). These journeys can involve opening one's heart to another person in a sacred marriage, the union of pairs of opposites. In mythology, when a god marries a goddess, each has found his or her other half. Marriage becomes the prime event in their lives; they give themselves, not to each other, but to the marriage. Another metaphysical outcome is the development of a special and loving relationship with God. For example, in the father-son atonement myth, the disciple envisions the father-god as having transcendent energy. Finally, some myths feature an experience of oneness with the universe. At this special moment, as described in the works of James Joyce (1993), the mythical voyager gains a new appreciation for the world. From this awesome experience, the hero gains a protective distance from the terror that exists in the world; at the same time he is able to experience compassion and joy in the moment. The wonder and awe of the universe have now spoken directly to the hero's soul and opened up a heightened appreciation of the mystery of life. This vision is beautifully captured in the Gospel according to Saint Thomas, where the Kingdom of God is described as being right in front of us, a vision that we do not usually see because of an enchantment of the eyes. The Christ figure disenchants us by opening our eyes. The Buddha also releases people from the enchantment of *Maya*, or illusion. These metaphysical journeys suggest that the world is a golden lotus, hidden only by the illusions woven by our own egos. By breaking through the ego limitations, one can behold paradise. These special journeys end at a place where desire and fear no longer operate, where one has a sense of compassion and empathy for the terror and suffering that are part of this world, and where one is free to experience the awe and mystery of the universe.

Campbell (1969) believed that the dynamism of energy systems within the body were the fertile foundation for mythology. From a sociological point of view, human beings preferred to live civilized and peaceful lives, but culture and society had laid only a thin veneer over the basic human physiology. Our heritage, the first vulnerability of aggression described in chapter 2, had imbued us with innate animalistic tendencies. Mythology could help human beings learn to accept these aspects of themselves as legacies of the primitive past. Rejection of these relics only alienates us from ourselves. Myths can help us integrate the many different sides of ourselves. The final stage, the metaphysical journey, is the most difficult. It requires coming to terms with the world of sorrow—the world of human beings attempting to act in civilized ways but often resorting to aggression as wild as that of any animal in the jungle. For Campbell, the solution to this dilemma was to be grounded in eternity. By realizing that the eternal was within, people could disengage and then reengage as joyful participants in the sorrows of the world.

At the completion of these mythical journeys, many people would have new perspectives on life. Fearing they might encounter cynicism and doubt, some may keep their sacred new beliefs to themselves after their journeys. Others may have difficulty communicating their new insights and, faced with an unsupportive world, find their new visions slowly disappearing. A few may recognize that the world is not ready to accept their new ideas but still persist in trying to share with humanity these vitalizing and energizing images.

Erikson (1959) has described the journey into middle adulthood and old age.[16] During the middle adult years, individuals must balance the impulse toward generativity, creative concern for the world and future generations, with the tendency toward stagnation. The final stage of life focuses on integrity versus despair. Integrity connotes a sense of peace with and acceptance of mortality and the human life cycle. Western and eastern images of the second part of life portray similar issues: making peace with mortality, finding meaning in life, and identifying the sacred within everyday experiences.

One of our greatest challenges as human beings is to serve as authentic guides, by honoring the journey of each individual, sharing our own vulnerabilities, being humble, and providing a loving context within which each person's mythical exploration can proceed. Mythology provides examples of the journeys that others have taken to become whole, to integrate the alienated parts of the self, and to learn to appreciate the wonder and mystery of life. Our greatest gift may be to help children and adolescents progress through initiation rites that are ennobling and meaningful.

THERAPY: NEW LESSONS IN HEALING

Our new paradigm must also include and build upon therapeutic theories and practices that make use of the legacy of spiritual traditions, foundational values, and mythological traditions. There are a number of problems that can be associated with the therapeutic enterprise as it is often practiced. Bellah et al. (1985) maintain that therapeutic relationships are usually distanced, circumscribed, and asymmetrical. These relationships focus on communicating and relating to others briefly and thus begin to resemble the superficial in other relationships in our complex society. If one's ultimate response to such a relationship is to wonder whether one is getting as much as one is giving—and if not, possibly to look for fulfillment elsewhere—then this contractual ethic leaves every commitment unstable. Constantly calculating the costs and benefits of relationships, with incessant renegotiations, is an awkward and unfulfilling way of relating to others. Lazarus (1985) adds that we often prescribe mechanical procedures best used to facilitate problem-focused coping with minor surface aspects of problems in living. For example, therapists sometimes help clients cope with adversity by teaching them to think positively and consider the clients who do not succeed at this technique ungrateful or resistant. This tendency to downplay the negative ends up trivializing authentic distress by denying its legitimacy.

The Need to Embrace the Dark Side

Cognitive behavioral interventions have been effectively employed to treat anxiety and depressive symptoms; such interventions can have many fewer negative side effects than the pharmacological interventions that medical personnel are inclined to dispense. However, the assumptions upon which many behavioral interventions are based may need to be reexamined. For example, cognitive behaviorists maintain that depressives' cognitions are pessimistic and distorted. Layne (1989) has found that depressives are more in touch with reality than supposedly normal subjects. Depressives' thoughts are painfully truthful, whereas nondepressives' thoughts are unrealistically positive. Layne suggests that "normals" have learned to erect a defensive screen against painful perceptions and that perhaps in our interventions for depressives we need to help them erect a defensive screen against reality. I suggest an alternative course. Rather than advocating defensive screens for both depressives and nondepressives, we need therapies that allow people to acknowledge, embrace, and make peace with the dark sides of life. We need to understand that the very real pain in life does not negate the simultaneous existence or possibility of joy and peace. By accepting and appreciating our vulnerabilities, we provide a firmer foundation for loving the life we have.

Therapy and the Quest for Meaning

As discussed earlier, profound discoveries in the sciences eventually influenced some of the leading philosophers and theorists to conclude that there is no God. At the beginning of this century, existentialism became a dominant force in western art, literature, theology, and philosophy. The existentialists challenged human beings to live lives of dignity, create their own internal self-worth, and take responsibility for the struggle of being against the possibility of not-being (May, 1960).

Frankl's (1983) approach, logotherapy, was based on the premise that therapy should facilitate the quest for meaning. Pleasure in life should not be the goal of our strivings; rather, it should be a side effect. Finding meaning in life can come through service to a higher cause or love for another person. Because human beings no longer learn what to do from traditions and traditional values, they increasingly find life empty and meaningless. Frankl believed that a new neurosis was springing from this existential frustration.

Maddi (1975) also described an existential neurosis, whose symptoms included a low-to-moderate activity level and a sense of meaninglessness, blandness, and boredom. Maddi believed that the premorbid personality of people who would eventually develop this neurosis was excessively concrete and fragmentary. Such people felt that they only played social roles and embodied biological needs. When confronted with recognition of this premorbid identity—through stresses such as the threat of death or disruptions of the social order—they would develop symptoms of existential neurosis. In contrast, people with healthy personalities were able to transcend social and biological living through active and uninhibited imagination. Acting and living with energy fueled by imagination, we can decide what we really want to do in the world and find the deeper meaning that exists beyond the realm of doing.

Peak Experiences and Flow States

The humanistic school helped focus mental health professionals on the more positive and uplifting aspects of human existence. Maslow (1962) believed that peak experiences were the moments of highest happiness and fulfillment. During these times, people paid total attention to what they were experiencing; their perceptions were richer, unselfish, and desireless. In this godlike state, existing outside time and space, a person's only emotions would be pity, charity, kindness, and sadness. Maslow believed that the self-actualization experience was a matter of degree and frequency, rather than an all-or-nothing event. This mystical experience has been described by people in every religion and culture.

In the popular book entitled *Flow*, Csikszentmihalyi (1990) describes the flow state as an optimal experience, in which people are so involved in an activity that nothing else seems to matter. He concludes that people feel most happy when they have learned to control their inner experiences. Csikszentmihalyi concludes that we can on rare occasions feel a sense of exhilaration and deep enjoyment, even in a cold and empty universe that is insensitive to human needs. He considers religions inadequate for providing permanent answers to coping with the lack of meaning in life. For Csikszentmihalyi, experiencing this optimal state is the foremost goal of every human being. He cites research indicating that people are in flow 54 percent of the time at work, and only 18 percent during leisure times, but that people would rather spend more time in leisure and less at work. While this finding that people spend more of their time in flow at work but prefer to spend more time in leisure represents a paradox for Csikszentmihalyi, it suggests a fundamental problem with his inclusive definition of flow. Social scientists should be careful to avoid transforming vital metaphors into concepts stripped of their deeper meaning, symbols, and history.

Humanist Therapies

Carl Rogers (1957) was one of the first to develop therapeutic methods based on humanistic beliefs, with an emphasis on understanding the client's phenomenological field. Rogers believed that therapists could best help their clients develop and grow by establishing therapeutic conditions of positive regard, unconditional acceptance, genuineness, and empathy. Gestalt therapy, developed by Fritz Perls (1973), also embraced the humanistic approach, with its emphasis on the here and now and its attempt to integrate the different parts of the self.

Humanist-oriented therapies have also flourished in the East. One of the more popular forms in Japan is called Morita therapy (Reynolds, 1984). Practitioners of Morita therapy offer clients a variety of meditative strategies, such as counting breaths, chanting mantras, and praying. This allows clients to constantly return to an awareness of their immediate circumstances. Morita therapists teach three key principles: accept your feelings, know your purpose, and do what needs to be done. Patients undergoing Morita therapy in Japan are often given one week's bed rest, so they can experience the waves of emotions coming and going. Slowly patients become more active, their attention directed toward completion of their job tasks. Hospitalization often lasts 40 to 60 days. Other Japanese therapies include Naikan, Shadan, and Seiza (Reynolds, 1980). These eastern therapies help clients develop their concentration and improve their health and stability of their character. Although Morita psychotherapy began in Japan in the early 1900s and clearly preceded the development of Perls' Gestalt therapy, there are a number of similarities between the two approaches. Both stress accepting your feelings as they are and then getting on with what needs to be done. Both emphasize the present—the "now."

In the mid-1970s, Ron Kurtz developed Hakomi body-centered psychotherapy, which was heavily influenced by Taoism and Buddhism (Johanson & Kurtz, 1991). Rather than analyzing and talking about life, clients are encouraged to turn their awareness toward the present moment, thus cultivating the state known in Buddhism as mindfulness. Clients practice staying with an experience—even negative emotions such as anxiety. As they report on their experience, it deepens, and "then one experience will lead to another and the process will move from surface experiences to core beliefs which generate and organize these experiences" (Johanson & Kurtz, 1991; p. 14).

Transpersonal Therapies

A number of other western therapies have spiritual dimensions; these are often called transpersonal therapies (Weide, 1973). In these approaches, the therapist uses traditional therapeutic techniques as well as meditation and other awareness exercises from the East (Mikulas, 1995; Vaughan, 1979). Clients learn to develop the capacity to take responsibility for themselves, to experience the full range of emotions while remaining detached from personal melodramas, and to meet their own physical, mental, and spiritual needs. Rather than curing ailments, the therapist's job is to help clients tap into their inner resources and let natural healing occur. Therapy is a process of awakening or becoming conscious. During the first stage of therapy—at the ego level—the client develops ego strength, raises self-esteem, and lets go of negative patterns of self-invalidation. At the second stage, ego death, the client stops identifying with roles, relationships, and possessions. Finally, at the stage of self-transcendence, the client realizes that he or she is just one part of a larger interrelated universe. The client's new qualities include an expanded sense of identity, increased compassion and inner peace, and a greater capacity for love and relatedness. When the therapeutic relationship is used to help the client find his or her path, it can be a transforming experience and journey.

In Louise L. Hay's (1993) tape recording *What I believe,* she states, "Love is the healing force, love dissolves anger, love releases guilt, love erases fear, love for ourselves is the power that heals us." People with affiliative trust, defined as a desire for loving relationships based on mutual respect, have been found to have fewer major illnesses (McKay, 1991). The Italian psychiatrist Assagioli (1965) would have concurred with this assessment. Assagioli believed that we wear masks for the roles we play (perfectionist, hero, victim, or judge) to obtain acknowledgment or attention, but that these masks are just expressions of the fear that we are not lovable—and that it is love that we really need.

Psychological therapies could be much more potent if they focused on teaching love and gratitude (Borysenko, 1993). Therapists would instruct clients to make lists of miracles in their lives that they take for granted, such as not being disabled or blind. Clients could also practice affirmations, such as "Bless my friends," for the good things in their lives. As in certain Tibetan Buddhist practices, visualizations could be used to send love to others. Practice in forgiving oneself and others could become a central focus of the healing process. Reframing problems to clarify choices and inspire spiritual optimism could be another technique in this transformative therapeutic process. Through prayer and meditation, clients could learn to change their lives by seeking peace and love. Like a shaman traveling to different parts of the soul that have been split off, tomorrow's spiritual healer will make soul mending a crucial part of therapy.

Regardless of their professional identification, effective therapists tend to be wise (Hanna and Ottens, 1995). Characteristics of wisdom in therapy include empathy (ability to understand others from their point of view), dialectical reasoning (recognition of the interplay of opposing views), tolerance of ambiguity, sagacity (self-knowledge and self-transcendence), deautomatization (resistance of the tendency toward automatic thought and behavior patterns), perspicacity (ability to intuitively understand and accurately interpret situations), metacognitive stance (recognition of the limits of knowledge and thinking), and skills in problem identification and problem solving. A therapist's possession of wisdom qualities may be a greater determinant of his or her effectiveness in helping clients than the specific theories or techniques followed. Schools of psychology and social work should consider developing courses on the acquisition and practice of wisdom qualities.

TECHNOLOGY IN SERVICE OF HUMANITY

Chapter 2 presented an analysis of many problems associated with the scientific and industrial revolutions. One advantage of the technologies stemming from these revolutions has been a decrease in the premium placed on male physical strength. With the introduction of machines that did not require physical strength to operate, the women's movement could emerge. With power less determined by strength, women's status improved, and they secured important legal rights to vote and own property.

George Orwell's and Aldous Huxley's depictions of the society of the future were presented in *1984* (Orwell, 1950) and *Brave New World* (Huxley, 1946). In the technologically driven societies depicted in these books, individual freedoms were suppressed by state-controlled, mindless citizens. Many have speculated whether our fascination with science and technology will inevitably lead us to barren outcomes. Buckminister Fuller (1975) was more optimistic when he suggested that some of our current crises might be amenable to alternative technologies that alter the physical environment in order to change our mental worlds.

The energy crisis is one of the most significant problems facing our species. We have destroyed vast stretches of land to find coal and oil; in burning these fuels, we have further damaged our fragile ecosystem. Some people support nuclear power, but we have not found effective ways to deal with the radioactive waste products. Inexpensive and abundant solar energy may represent the most promising technological solution, however. Thus in the development of power sources, technology was initially part of the problem but one day might be transformed into part of the solution.

Computers are becoming an integral part of our lives. As the new "Information Superhighway" becomes a reality, more people will begin working in their homes, thereby lessening the need to commute to work in congested cities. People who work at home should have more time to spend with their families and on leisure activities. Gardens could replace some of the office buildings in our crowded cities. For the past two hundred years, there has been an unnatural concentration of people in cities; the Information Revolution could facilitate the spread of the population back to small towns and cities, which form healthier and more natural arrangements than urban metropolises. Adequate planning for this migration could help us avoid the gutting and abandonment of inner cities that followed some past technological advances.

In Howard Rheingold's book *The Virtual Community* (1995), we see a new vision for interactive technologies, with computers being used to put people in touch with each other over the entire world. Today hundreds of conferences occur regularly through computer bulletin boards, and in ten years these conferences will include not only text but also video images. Some conferences have brought people together to network or work collaboratively on community problems. Rather than passively watching television, people can be more active by holding discussions on computer networks. There are dangers to the user, however: spending too much time with multimedia devices, relying on inaccurate information, and being exposed to pornographic material.

Present-day supercomputers are not as powerful as a honeybee's brain, which has one million neurons and performs approximately ten billion operations per second. A human being's brain has 100 billion neurons, a number 100,000 times greater than that of the honeybee's brain. These 100 billion neurons are connected to combine power, and these billions of neurons form 100 trillion connections. There are more connections in a single human brain than there are particles in the universe. Supercomputers are based on serial processing, whereas the brain uses parallel distributed processing (Tryon, 1995). Patterns of neuronal activation form representations, and every experience, every image refers to a pattern of activities across neurons.

In future generations, when supercomputers surpass the capacity of the human brain, the world of technology will present new opportunities and challenges to our way of life. Science fiction novels and movies have shown us many devastating scenarios for the possible outcome of this advance. It is possible that, instead, future supercomputers will represent an evolutionary progression, helping people reach a higher consciousness and a greater appreciation for life and wisdom.

Some futurists believe that one day we will be able to design small computers that rearrange atoms and that these computers will then be able to make all the products we need. Nanotechnology is the term used to describe the production of tiny machines the size of viruses. It is predicted that nanotechnology will enable us to make many production machines with almost no pollution and at minimal cost. These machines would be able to eliminate all diseases. They would produce all manufactured goods. We would then have to find something else to do with our time. Could our scientific prowess provide the luxury to free ourselves from the need to manufacture? Whether this new society will provide comfort for all, or for only a select few, will depend on who controls it and on the checks and balances installed to guard against abuses of power. The supercomputers of the future could be new "life forms," helping and guiding us to a saner and more balanced existence. The possibilities for such a future are intriguing and in some ways daunting.

Technology may not be our enemy, but it must be tempered by values that sustain life and nature. Values and rituals have the capacity to guide and heal and can provide a sense of identity and meaning. Some of the values of the urban, industrial West have led to the destruction of the ecological health of our planet. In the past, rich values and traditions helped regulate our relationships with the earth and prevented destruction of our habitat. Beatrice Briggs (1993) suggests that the values, stories, and rituals we need now "redirect our attention to the earth, remind us of the beauty and mystery of creation, and make clear our utter dependence on the planet's air, soil, water, seeds, and other species for our survival" (p. 36).

4

Religion and Spirituality

> [P]lease, find a way. Find a way beyond the continuous chain reaction of craving, jealousy, ill will, indifference, fear, and anxiety that fills the mind. Find a way that dissolves the deeply ingrained patterns of negative, distrustful behavior caused by past cruelty and disappointment. Find a way that demonstrates to you that ill will and greed are damaging to your psyche. Find a way that grounds your deeds in wisdom, equanimity, compassion, and loving kindness. Find a way that reveals to you the joy of our profound unity, the subtle interrelatedness of you and every being, every manifestation of the unfolding universe. Find a way that will continually deepen your understanding of that knowledge. Then we could build community without hypocrisy. Then we would have a chance.
>
> —Charlene Spretnak
> *States of Grace*

CONTEMPORARY PSYCHOLOGY: PERSPECTIVES ON SPIRITUALITY

The Study of Wisdom

Greeley (1974) maintains that one of the great heresies of the western world has been our reliance on knowledge taken only from discursive or cognitive sources. The study of wisdom (the capacity to cope with uncertainty, the ability to frame an event in its larger context) provides knowledge from other sources. Staudinger, Smith, and Baltes (1992) summarized literature suggesting that with age performance on fluid intelligence tasks decreases but that some crystallized properties of intelligence, like wisdom, show age-related stability or even growth.[17] We may become nicer people as we age, substituting tolerance, moderation, and balance for impulsiveness and dogmatism.

Research on mystical experiences has also produced insights into the complicated domain of wisdom. Psychiatric explanations of mystical experiences have suggested that many of these phenomena can be interpreted as states of regression to infancy or even symptoms of schizophrenia. Greeley (1974) disputes this interpretation, citing the work of William James, who characterized mystical experiences as ineffable (defying expression), noetic (producing an overwhelming experience of clarity), transient, and passive (creating the feeling that one has been grasped by a superior power). Greeley (1974) and Hay and Morisy (1978) report that from one-third to one-half of the population have had mystical experiences, although Thomas and Cooper (1978) suggest that many of these experiences should not be defined as mystical.[18]

The Functions of Religion

Spirituality and mysticism are often associated with religious experiences. Advocates of religion have suggested that these experiences provide direction and comfort and encourage altruistic behavior, whereas skeptics accuse religions of appealing to infantile security needs and providing easy answers to difficult questions (Batson & Ventis, 1982). Spilka, Hood, and Gorsuch (1985) state that religion is a complex, multidimensional phenomenon and that for most people religion is mechanical and dogmatic: Basic religious beliefs are not to be questioned. For some people, however, religion can sponsor growth and personal enrichment. In a broad review of the literature, Payne, Bergin, Bielema, and Jenkins (1991) indicate that there is a positive relationship between religiosity and subjective sense of well-being. In addition, intrinsic religious orientation is associated with healthy psychological characteristics, and extrinsic religious orientation is associated with maladjustment. People with intrinsic religiosity are unselfish and find their master motive in religion (Allport & Ross, 1967). In contrast, those with an extrinsic orientation use religion for their own aims: to attain status, security, and self-justification. Pargament and Maton (in press) suggest that religious participation can have a positive impact on mental health by fulfilling the need for a sense of meaning (which helps reassure people that life will work out at some point); the need for community and belonging (which helps people feel that they are not alone in their struggles); and the need for proactive involvement in improving the world (which heightens feelings of empowerment by showing people that they can make changes in the world and help others).

Theories of Spiritual Development

Fowler (1982) has delineated six stages of spiritual development, borrowing from Piaget and Kohlberg's stages of cognitive and moral development. Although Fowler's work is complex and lacks empirical research (Spilka, Hood, & Gorsuch, 1985), it provides some interesting schema for understanding potential religious pathways. Peck (1987) has condensed these concepts into a sequence of four stages. Stage 1 is called Chaotic and Antisocial. People at this level are unprincipled and selfish. Although they may pretend to be loving, in fact they are incapable of empathic responses to others. At this stage of underdeveloped spirituality, they are basically manipulative and self-serving. Stage 2 is called Formal and Institutional, and it is the stage of the majority of churchgoers. They are attached to the forms of their religions, and most have visions of God as an external, judging, rule-giving being. Stage 3 is called Skeptic and Individual. At this stage, people reject formal religious life, although many remain committed to social causes. Stage 4 is called Mystical and Communal. At this phase, the seeker experiences the underlying unity and interconnectedness of all things.

Humanity is struggling to attain a higher level of consciousness, and people who show potential for higher states of consciousness often have qualities associated with the most spiritually advanced people (Ring, 1984). Whether they have undergone religious or spiritual experiences, near-death experiences, or chronic illness, many people have awakened within themselves the potential for experiencing and responding to the world in entirely new ways. They have found pathways that are more complete, peaceful, appreciative, and constructive.

Categories of Spiritual Experience

There have been several attempts to devise systems to categorize wisdom from a cognitive point of view or to order religious experiences, often taking into account personal experiences. A different approach has been proposed by Berry (1988), Wegela (1988), and Burkhardt (1989).

Thomas Berry (1988) identified three basic patterns of the universe: differentiation, subjectivity, and communion. Differentiation describes the variety of life in our world; by attending to this process, we gain greater appreciation of the enormous creativity before us. Subjectivity refers to a person's unique interior depth and spontaneity. Finally, communion implies relationships, interrelatedness, and the development of community. Actions that are in accord with these three processes are considered ethical and wholesome.

Wegela (1988) identified three aspects of health from a Buddhist point of view: spaciousness, clarity, and warmth. These aspects have elements in common with Berry's conceptualizations. Spaciousness, which is similar to Berry's pattern of differentiation, is an accommodation to whatever experiences arise within. Clarity is a full apprehension, without embellishment, of the textures, temperatures, and colors of one's experiences. Finally, warmth, which is similar to Berry's communion, is an experience of compassion for oneself and others. One can bring these qualities to any experience, and in doing so, one experiences intrinsic health. Regardless of external condition or physical difficulties, health is always within us if we are open to these experiences. The purpose of the healer is to uncover what already exists.

Burkhardt (1989) identified three characteristics of spirituality: inner strength, sense of meaning in life, and harmonious interconnectedness. Through inner strength, people find an animated sense of joy and peace within their inner wellspring of awareness. By finding a meaning in life, people discover a sense of hope in the unfolding mystery, uncertainty, and ambiguity of life and an ability to see beyond the present realities. The last characteristic, interconnectedness, is a process of finding harmony with the self, others, and the universe.

Measurement of Foundational Values

Jason, Reichler et al. (1997) recently developed the Foundational Values Scale, a test designed to measure these dimensions as perceived in the life of another person. The five dimensions of this scale tap the different components of wisdom. The first component, Harmony, consists of items assessing balance, self-love, good judgment, appreciation, and purpose in life. These are internal domains; they tap some components of Berry's pattern of subjectivity, Wegela's aspect of spaciousness, and Burkhardt's characteristic of finding a purpose in life. People who are balanced, appreciate life, and can cope with uncertainty tend to be less burdened by stress. The second component of the Foundational Values Scale, Warmth, includes kindness, compassion, and animation. This domain is related to Berry's pattern of communion, Wegela's aspect of warmth, and Burkhardt's characteristic of harmonious interconnectedness. The qualities of kindness and compassion appear to be related to being in the present and having a sense of humor. People with these qualities can extend hope and happiness to others. The third component of the scale is Intelligence. It is not merely the quality of intelligence, but how it is used, that determines its connection to wisdom. Using one's intelligence to solve problems and help others is a key feature of wisdom-related intelligence. The fourth component, Nature, consists of a concern and reverence for the environment and a sense that all life is interconnected. This domain is closely related to Berry's pattern of differentiation and Wegela's aspect of spaciousness. One component of perceived wisdom is concern for the environment. This component is also related to the experience of flow; love and appreciation of the external world helps people become so deeply involved in an activity that nothing else seems to matter. This dimension is reflected in foundational knowledge as practiced by Native Americans, who have revered and remained in balance with nature for thousands of years (Spretnak, 1991). The final component, Spirituality, consists of living a spiritual life and having a fellowship or union with God.

SPIRITUAL TRADITIONS: EIGHT EXAMPLES

Systems of identifying spirituality and wisdom are interesting and useful. However, it is important to remember that the essence of spirituality cannot be captured in any system of thought. Many believe that it cannot be captured at all by human minds, only apprehended with greater or lesser certainty as experiences more of the heart than of the mind. All we can do is describe our experiences, study whatever has been written, and look to a number of spiritual traditions.

Many religions have dealt with these higher domains of human consciousness. It is to them that we may look for moral guidance and inspiration toward a better understanding of health, love, and a sense of community. In this chapter, several religions are presented as illustrations of the healing, powerful messages within rich cultural traditions. Many themes within religion have been used for inappropriate purposes: war, oppression, or financial gain. Nevertheless, most religions contain vital, energizing symbols and messages that can help restore a sense of meaning to those who are alienated; rekindle love for others in those whose hearts have grown weary; reaffirm the beauty of the natural, external world for those who have become jaded by materialism; and resuscitate an inner sense of joy and peace in those whose minds have long dwelled on negative obsessions. The following are by no means the only examples of religions whose symbols and messages can promote healing.

Hinduism

Neki (1975) characterizes much of western philosophy as emphasizing subject/object dualism, whereas in the East there is no such distinct cleavage. The ideal for mental health in the West is the creation of harmony between subject and object, an adjustment of the self to the environment. Western ideals focus on developing an adequate perception of reality and mastering the environment. Eastern approaches, such as Hinduism, consider our perceptions of reality to be illusionary and believe that environmental mastery breeds imbalance and excessive pride. In

Hinduism there is an emphasis on intrapsychic harmony, freedom from otherness, and liberation from the bondage of the mind.

Western readers might reject these ideas that originated in India, because they associate that country with dire poverty and sexist practices: Families sometimes abort female children, and some adolescent girls are sold into marriage. However, even if one disapproves of some current practices within a country, it is still possible to recognize and value important ideas that have their origins in that culture.

A goal for Hindus is to reach a state of *samadhi*. People who reach this state have attained illumination, equipoise, spontaneity, freedom, and harmony. Illumination is a state of appreciation and a sense of enjoyment without sensual urges, which is sustained by the ending of thought processes. Equipoise consists of the cessation of emotional turbulence, with pleasures and pains passing like changes of garments. Spontaneity is all that one does naturally, without effort. Freedom is a state without desire, greed, envy, jealousy, or hostility. Harmony is an awareness of the inner balance and peace that pervades the cosmos.

India had a highly evolved civilization at about 2000 B.C. The Indo-European invasions brought about a crisis in the culture, and a caste system subsequently elevated the lighter-skinned invaders to the rank of Brahmin, while the darker-skinned natives were assigned to lower castes (Campbell, 1980). In the Vedas, written about 1000 B.C., the Brahmins, as priests, were assigned the role of interpreting the holy books. These priests were thought to be in touch with the energy of the world. In addition, a completely new idea was introduced: that an illuminated person had greater powers and wisdom than any god in the universe. These and other ideas were further developed in the Upanishads, written about 800 B.C., which taught that it is not necessary to seek help from the Brahmins for enlightenment because the source of God is within our own hearts. The deities of the Hindu religion are symbolic of the energies of the self (Campbell, 1980). These holy texts pointed to eternal forces of mystery that transcended all definitions and categories, and they were intended to help people experience that mystery.

The Hindus believed that *prana*, or psychic energy, both encompasses and extends beyond electrical, magnetic, and radioactive energy. This energy force field surrounds the body, radiating up to 12 feet. There are three types of energy flow (*nadis*): *pingala*, *ida*, and *sushumna*. *Pingala* is the basic energy of life. It includes the action mode, the sympathetic nervous system, the achievement of goals, and the pursuit of social rewards. It is associated with yang—masculine and dynamic energy. *Ida*'s energy is inwardly directed. It includes the receptive mode, the parasympathetic nervous system, decreases in muscle tone, and states of inaction. It is associated with yin—feminine and receptive energy. The third force is *sushumna*, or spiritual energy. For centuries yogis have claimed that imbalances in the *nadis* (especially in *ida* and *pingala*) would cause disease, and that their techniques could rectify these imbalances. In Satyananda Saraswati's book *Kundalini Tantra* (1984), he described the work of Hiroshi Motoyama of Japan. Motoyama developed a machine to measure the waves and currents of energy that accompany an awakening of *Kundalini* (the serpent-like life force rising from the bottom to the top of the body). He found that if one's *ida* or *pingala* energy system was underactive or overactive, this imbalance would predispose one to disease.

Disciples of yoga use a variety of strategies to achieve oneness with the divine energy. The egoless experience can result in a state of calm, detachment, and nonintention. The steps of yoga include following an ethical code, practicing certain body postures, voluntary self-regulation of respiration, and concentration or meditation practices. Goyeche (1977) considers yoga a way of life, whose medical benefits are considered side-effects. As tension is relieved, people often experience gross somatic discharges (muscle spasms). Stretching of the muscles produces proprioceptive stimulation, which is responsible for optimal muscle tone and can help produce an optimal state of hypothalamic and autonomic balance. Ultimately, the reduction of proprioception can reduce the responsiveness of the hypothalamus and diminish hypothalamic-cortical discharge (Goyeche, 1977).

To move *prana* through the body circuits, Hindus use a variety of yoga strategies. These practices aim to expand the mind and liberate energy—to yoke waking consciousness with pure consciousness (Chaudhuri, 1975). Hatha yoga involves breathing and body exercises to make the body healthy and strong. In Karma yoga one learns to selflessly accept life's duties and act without desire or fear as an agent of the divine. This work, which is not attached to materialistic strivings, is performed as a devotion to God and an opportunity to learn and live a spiritual life. Jnana yoga is a process of developing mental disciplines to gain greater understanding of the higher realities of life. Mental discriminations, which comprise one type of mental discipline, often involve the objects and subjects of knowledge. For example, disciples might practice the thoughts, I am not my body; I am just a witness. Bhakti yoga focuses on devoting all activities to attaining self-surrender and love for a god, an animal, or a person. While one is worshiping an external force, one is really becoming devoted to a divine aspect of oneself. Kundalini yoga attempts to awaken the vital, serpent-like life force within our bodies. Mantra yoga is a process of meditating on certain sounds to attain self-purification. Finally, Raja yoga is an eight-step path toward becoming one with the higher self. Its goal is to stop the spontaneous workings of the mind. This is often illustrated by the image of a pond whose water is rippling in the blowing wind. By making the wind stop—by quieting the mind—one can calm the water and see images of perfect form.

Buddhism

Buddhism focuses on the death of the ego. Buddhists believe that suffering stems from unrealistic expectations in an impermanent world. The goal is to achieve transcendence and to be freed of desire and fear, in order to participate in this turbulent and sorrowful world with joy and rapture (Campbell, 1980). Through 227 observances and prohibitions, followers of this religion restrain their actions so they can achieve a calm and subdued mind. To control the mind, Buddhists employ the technique of mindfulness, a process that requires restraint of the senses. To facilitate detachment from internal thoughts and perceptions, Buddhists cultivate the habit of noticing sensory perceptions but not letting them stimulate the mind into chain reactions of thoughts. The Buddha taught that when the conscious mind perceived a stimulus, it would assign a positive or negative value to it, and then negative or positive sensations would arise in the body, depending on the intensity of the valuation (Spretnak, 1991). Deep levels of the unconscious mind would then react to these bodily sensations by generating pleasant or unpleasant emotions. Simple awareness of subtle sensations, without judging them as bad or good, can eradicate patterns of response that might otherwise cause deep complexes.

Beginning Buddhists often find it difficult to fix their minds on a single object without being distracted by thoughts. The mind processes 126 bits of information per second, 7,560 per minute (Csikszentmihalyi, 1990). Trying to calm and slow down this overactive processing takes discipline and perseverance. The conscientious student will initially reach the access stage, where there are moments of overcoming the hindering thoughts; this is accompanied by feelings of rapture, happiness, and equanimity (Goleman, 1992). At this stage, some people experience flashes of light or feel as if they are floating in air. At the next level, called the first *Jhana*, awareness of painful body states and sensory perceptions vanishes. This experience lasts for only a second, but in the next four stages one gradually experiences longer periods of one-pointedness and equanimity. At the highest levels of consciousness (beginning with Nirvana), all attachment to ego and desire is extinguished. At the final stage (*Nirodh*), awareness ceases altogether.

These are two schools of Buddhism: Mahayana and Therevada (also referred to as Hinayana). The Therevada approach is monastic and focuses on renunciation of the world in the hope of attaining enlightenment. The Mahayana school is more active in efforts to bring change into the external world. An example of the Mahayana approach is Zen Buddhism. Members of the Zen school focus on practicing *zazen*. In this meditation, the conscious mind is quieted and the unconscious is liberated.

The mind returns to the ultimate reality of the void or emptiness that contains all (Owens, 1992).

Buddhists believe that life is full of experiences that produce suffering. In the first of the Four Noble Truths, the Buddha taught that suffering can be experienced as a result of birth, old age, sickness, death, separation from loved ones, desire, attachment, and clinging. In the Second Noble Truth, the cause of suffering is attributed to attachment and desire, which inflame anger, jealousy, grief, worry, and despair. The Third Noble Truth is that understanding the truth about life brings about the cessation of suffering. The Fourth Noble Truth is the path that leads to the cessation of suffering (Nhat Hanh, 1991). Suffering can be eliminated only through the Eightfold Noble Path: rightness in speech, action, and livelihood (morality); rightness in concentration, mindfulness, and effort (meditation); and rightness in understanding and thought (wisdom). During meditation, the disciple progresses through the various levels of the unconscious. At the first level, imagery, the meditator sees countless, apparently meaningless, images. At the next level, neurosis, a person may relive painful childhood problems. At the historic and symbolic level, one sees images from history that are symbolic. Finally, at the self-realization level, one undergoes religious experiences.

For several hundreds of years, Tibet existed as a peaceful and spiritual country, ruled by a Buddhist leader, the Dalai Lama. Although currently controlled by China, the Tibetan people provide an example of how people can live together in peace and deep connection with their land and traditions. In the future countries may be established to achieve goals that are more spiritual than economic.

Judaism

A large portion of the laws in the Torah (the first five books of the Bible) prohibit injustices and inhumanities. Exploitation and evil are seen as violations of the community's special relationship with God. In spite of considerable inter-religious warfare, the religions of the West have a strong social ethic prescribing that one help one's neighbor and eliminate injustice in the world. This strong social ethic is more highly developed in western religions than in eastern religions (Spretnak, 1991). Judaism also produced the first consistent ethical codes based on true monotheism (Upshur, Terry, Holoka, Goff, & Lowry, 1991).

Jewish mysticism has its roots in the Bible. The Jewish mystic, unlike the Hindu mystic, never sought complete absorption or loss of separate identity. There was always a relationship between the subject and God, the awesome and majestic King. Epstein (1959) describes Jewish mysticism as messianic, in that it posits an ongoing struggle for redemption from evil and the coming of a Messiah who will one day restore the world to a state of harmony. The sinfulness of man began with Adam's disobedience; the perfect unity was then broken and evil appeared. People were created to restore the original unity and thereby revive the unimpeded flow of divine love.

Jewish mysticism, or the kabbalah, includes books such as the Zohar, Sefer Yezirah, and the Hasidic literature. Kabbalah has been practiced since the eleventh century; it was at first a secret doctrine for a privileged few. It developed along two distinct lines, the practical (the German school) and the speculative (the Provence-Spanish school) (Epstein, 1959). Practical mysticism focused on cultivating the constant sense of God's presence through prayer, inner meditation, and contemplation, in order to obtain a vision of *Kabod*, God's divine light. In this pursuit of the pure love of God, practitioners had to remember their duties to the community. The Jews in Germany, oppressed and persecuted, turned to these teachings as a means of escape from their miseries.

The Jews of Provence and Spain were more fortunate during the twelfth through fifteenth centuries, and they were more attracted to the speculative side of the kabbalah. Their aim was to discover the hidden mysteries contained in every word and letter in the Bible. Around 1300, the Zohar was compiled from various sources by Moses de Leon of Granada, and it soon became the textbook of Jewish mystics (Epstein, 1959). This text was intended to reveal the hidden meaning of the biblical narratives. It taught that the study of Torah was one of the foremost duties of a Jew, and that prayer practiced with devotion can result in the descent of peace and joy upon the person praying, and upon others. In study and prayer, one learns that in love can be found the secret of divine unity.

According to the Zohar, God made His existence perceptible by projecting ten channels of light, called the *sefiroth*. There are many similarities between the Indian *chakras* and the Jewish *sephirot*, the ten energy centers in the body derived from the *sefiroth*, the luminous rays that God poured forth at creation. According to Blank (1993), the highest *sephirah* (*keter*) corresponds to the seventh *chakra*, representing God's essence. The second and third *sephirot* (*hokhman* and *binah*) correspond to the sixth *chakra*. *Hokhman* is active, yang, masculine power; whereas *binah* is receptive, yin, intuitive power; each balances the other in harmonious opposition. The fourth and fifth *sephirot* (*hesed* and *gevurah*) correspond to the fifth *chakra*. *Hesed* is God's nurturing love, and *gevurah* is the power of God to move one to action. The sixth *sephirah* (*tiferet*) rests at the heart. The seventh and eighth *sephirot* represent dominance (*nezah*) and submissiveness (*hod*); these opposites sometimes struggle. The ninth *sephirah* (*yesod*) corresponds to the genital *chakra*, and the lowest *sephirah* (*malkhut*) corresponds to the physical world that contains only hints of the spiritual world.

The Zohar captured the hearts and minds of Jews, and after the expulsion of the Jews from Spain in 1492, it became a fresh source of strength, filling them with spiritual power (Epstein, 1959). The exiles carried the Zohar to countries throughout Europe and the Middle East. It was at Safed in Palestine that the Zoharic teachings reached their highest state. For example, Moses Cordovero taught that the infinite is present in every part of the finite; this belief is similar to the pantheism taught a century later by Spinoza. The sixteenth-century Jewish mystic Rabbi Issac Luria elaborated theoretical Zoharic principles. He claimed that the holy sparks of God's light infuse everything but that its sparks are hidden by distractions, obstacles, and confusions. The Safed mystics believed that through study, prayer, and devotional exercises they could speed up the return of the Messiah. During these centuries, the kabbalah was still restricted to the circles of the learned. It was not until the eighteenth century, with the rise of Hasidism, that these ideas and doctrines were brought to the Jewish masses (Shapiro, 1989).

There remains today a strong mystical element within several sects of Judaism, including those from the Hasidic traditions as well as a more recent movement called P'nai Or, a number of current Jewish mystical techniques focus on quieting the mind, letting in the "still small voice of God," reciting wordless melodies, visualizing the name of God, conversing with God, and focusing on nothingness (Shapiro, 1989).

Christianity

Mysticism and deep levels of spirituality have periodically risen within the Christian religions for two thousand years. In lower Egypt in 1945, 13 Gnostic texts were discovered. They had been written in the second century and buried during the third or fourth century. These early Christian texts stressed the inner journey toward the divine (Kenny, 1991). Salvation was thought to come not through the Church or the sacraments but rather from finding the divine spark within. The widespread Gnostic communities of the second century believed in poverty and chastity and took a dim view of sexuality. They considered women the spiritual equals of men. By the fourth century, these early Gnostics were persecuted by the Church, and most of their books were burned.

In the Middle Ages, the movement toward mysticism was revived and spread through Italy, France, and Germany (Kenny, 1991). In the 1200s, this movement was seen as a threat to the Church, because the Gnostics believed that Church officials could not tell them what to do; rather, they believed that each person had to find his or her own beliefs and inner teachings. Pope Innocent III began the Inquisition to root out the Gnostic heresy.

The third appearance of Gnostic ideas occurred in the Renaissance in the mid–1400s. When the Turks came to power in the eastern portion of the old Roman Empire, a flood of books from the East came into Italy (Kenny, 1991). The hermetic sciences of astrology and alchemy became known to some of the leading thinkers of this time. Written in the third century by scholars in Alexandria, hermetic books stressed that human beings could transcend their daily predicaments by using the mind to reach enlightenment. These were powerful ideas; they represented a new form of humanism, one that viewed human beings as filled with wonder and capable of anything. Science could be used to look closely at everything, including the human body. These humanistic ideas—affirming that to be human was divine—were born of the same impulses as the Gnostic ideas. The Church once again began to persecute people who subscribed to hermetic ideas.

The fourth great revitalization of the Gnostic tradition began in this century. After the discovery of the Gnostic texts in 1945, Jung spent much of his remaining life reading and studying these materials. For him, the languages of all dreams and myths were similar, and these archetypical materials were richly portrayed in the Gnostic gospels (Kenny, 1991).

Today, the Christian mystic's deepest form of religious experience is the realization of union with God. The ordinary duties of life are seen as part of self-discipline. The three phases of a mystic's life are purification (purging of self-centeredness), illumination (fellowship with God), and union (self-transformation as part of the mystical body of God). The Christian mystics attempt to develop their full humanness by being decent human beings; this state renders them more capable of plumbing their mystical depths. Growth of perfect charity entails loving God first, then one's neighbor. Prayer is considered a delight, for through prayer one experiences the presence of God. Asceticism requires detachment from little desires, so that one can concentrate on the one all-encompassing desire, the desire for God. Silence and solitude allow one to experience the presence of God (McNamara, 1992).

O'Hanlon (1981) has noted similarities between Christian and eastern practices. In both, the true self awakens when the surface mind and disordered desires are stilled. Through prayer or through watching one's breath, observing sensations, or repeating mantras, one can experience deeper stages of mystical experience.

Perhaps the most well-known Christian mystic was Thomas Merton. In his autobiography, Merton (1948) noted that in our materialistic society, worldly success depends on the applause of others, as if this is the only way to feel real. In contrast, at his Trappist monastery, the best people attracted the least attention. Merton detached himself from the world in order to lead a contemplative life. According to Merton, one can be filled with peace and gratitude by loving God and devoting oneself to a life of service. His poignant message is well summed up in the following passage:

> Virtues are precisely the powers by which we can come to acquire happiness. Without them, there can be no joy because they are the habits which coordinate and canalize our natural energies and direct them to the harmony, perfection and balance of the unity of our nature with itself and with God, which must in the end constitute our everlasting peace.

Islam

The religion of Al-Islam was established among the Arabians in the early part of the seventh century by the Prophet Muhammed. Although Islam permits its followers to have different understandings of Islamic concepts, modern Muslims have split into a number of schisms and cults whose differences far exceed the differences permitted. The Islamic belief mandates all Muslims to worship The One God (Allah) as a unified community (the *Ummah*) and to base their concepts upon teachings from the Quran and Hadith.

The faith of Al-Islam outlines a comprehensive framework within which Muslims can worship God in each aspect of their lives. The Prophet Muhammed formulated the religion as a spiritual guide for all facets of human existence. For practicing Muslims, Al-Islam provides meticulous descriptions of the proper methods for prayer rituals, personal conduct, domestic roles, professional endeavors, economic systems, political structures, and social involvement.

Faith in Al-Islam is intended to instill justice and equity as the fundamental principles in the Muslim lifestyle. Western media have often failed to distinguish the glaring discrepancies between Muslim teachings and the practices that have been branded fanatical, sexist, and antiquated. Yet the religion of Al-Islam forbids Muslims to participate in any discriminatory practices, including the subordination of women and arranged marriages that are prevalent in certain segments of Arab and Muslim societies.

The fundamental principles of practice in Al-Islam are manifested in the Five Pillars of Faith: (1) to bear witness that there is no deity except Allah and that Muhammed is the Messenger of Allah; (2) to observe the five daily prayers; (3) if one's financial resources exceed a specified minimum, to pay 2.5 percent of one's earnings into an annual *Zakat* that is distributed among financially needy people; (4) to fast during the month of Ramadan; and (5) to perform a pilgrimage (*hajj*) to Mecca at least once in a lifetime.

The perspectives on justice in Al-Islam have enabled the religion to play a major role in social reformation throughout history. After its establishment in Arabia, Al-Islam dramatically changed Arabia into one of the most productive and advanced civilizations of its era. Muslims' meticulous study and implementation of their religion allowed Arab society to implement social reforms, including the abolition of liquor, gambling, slavery, prostitution, superstition, discrimination, and all forms of self-indulgence.

With these changes, the Islamic civilization in Arabia assumed a vanguard position in social enlightenment and development. The Muslims' commitment to piety and knowledge became a catalyst for significant contributions to the fields of science, culture, and religion. Arab contributions spread to Europe, influencing the great revival of arts and sciences that became known as the Renaissance.

Within Islam, Sufism is the most mystical school or spiritual path. The aim of Sufism is to open oneself to "high knowledge," "deep understanding," or wisdom (Ornstein, 1992). Practitioners of Sufism believe that questions such as What is the meaning of life? cannot be answered systematically through the rational mind but must be approached through experiential knowledge. The Sufi mission is to help people awaken and start their journey toward living the present life in all its fullness. In the quest to develop their true permanent part, their slogan is to "Be in the world, but not of the world."

There is no dogma or fixed system in Sufism. What is appropriate to open one's eyes in one civilization may not be appropriate in another. In Sufi teaching tales provide lessons. A sage may play the part of an ordinary man, and in the story the reader may follow an unexpected course and end with a better ability to understand the limitations in contemporary social customs.

In Sufism, one need be neither vegetarian nor celibate. One need not give up one's current identity; rather, the stories urge practitioners to "wake up." The awakened person remains active in the world.

Native American Spirituality

For more than 20,000 years, Native American nations have maintained an earth-based spirituality that has attempted to attain harmony and balance with the laws of nature (Spretnak, 1991). Because the world was seen as suffused with spiritual powers, interactions with it were always respectful. Communal ceremonies bound communities together by helping their members remain in balance with the universe, maintain an attitude of respect and gratitude, and fulfill their obligations to the land.

Shamans are integral parts of many Native American traditions, as well as the traditions of cultures in South America, Africa, and Asia. Shamanism began with the early hunters and gatherers, and it never died out. Shamanism is not a religion, and it has no formal priesthood or dogma (Heinze, 1990). Shamans are in touch with the spiritual dimension, but they are always humble. They see themselves not as healers but as guides. A shaman can see three levels of reality: the earth, the regions below the earth, and the regions above. The shaman can regularly travel to the realms above and below the earth, meet with spirits, and bring knowledge back to earth (Walsh, 1990). Shamans have an ecological sense of the world: they see everything we do affecting everything else on a planet where all is interconnected and whole. While the behavior of shamans during their journeys might lead some to consider them psychotic, their perceptions are not agitated or disturbed; rather, they can control their states of mind, they experience good concentration, and they have a coherent sense of self (Walsh, 1990).

Missionaries during the sixteenth century and beyond worked to eradicate indigenous religious practices in North, Central, and South America and attempted to convert the people to Christianity. In the Native American religions, as well as in the African religions, there is no separation between the secular and the sacred. Rather, the whole of existence is considered a religious phenomenon.

African Religions

Sharing the wisdom of her native West Africa, Some (1995) describes how many African boys and girls go through religious initiation rites. During these ceremonies, drumming helps adolescents enter the spirit world. After they return from this experience, the participants are changed in nature, for they have entered and seen a new reality. They have a sense of previous lives and are better able to rid themselves of useless traits, behaviors, and attitudes.

The indigenous religious world has an intensity and aliveness that is beyond intellectual knowledge; this experience is hinted at in the African saying, "The thing that knowledge can not eat." Elders in a village do not explain people, objects, or events; rather, they say "Learn by watching." There is another African saying, "It takes a village to raise a child," a phrase that has been used often in this country in recent years, as a slogan and program title. We have much to learn from this perspective that suggests that religious life and values need to be woven into the entire fabric of the community for our wisdom, teachings, and traditions to be passed on to future generations.

This collectivist creed—putting the needs of the ethnic group before one's own needs—is worth honoring and restoring. Many African Americans in this culture face the choice between self-oriented American individualism and African-derived collectivist strivings. Gaines and Reed (1995) maintain that, when African Americans assume that the personality of the dominant culture is the ideal norm, that assumption sets the stage for a number of dysfunctional patterns. The principles of Kwanzaa, an African-American celebration developed by Maulana Karenga based on traditional African values, represent a contemporary effort to promote the psychological health and strength of African Americans by affirming these deeply rooted cultural values. The seven principles of Kwanzaa (the *Nguzo Saba*) are *Umoja* (unity), *Kujichagulia* (self-determination), *Ujima* (collective work and responsibility), *Ujamaa* (cooperative economics), *Nia* (purpose), *Kuumba* (creativity), and *Imani* (faith).

Liberation Theology

Arising within African and Latin American contexts, liberation theologists interpret the Christian Gospel as a call for justice and liberation from oppression. Leading spokespersons for this movement, including Paulo Friere and Dom Helder Camara of Brazil, Gustavo Gutierrez of Peru, and Juan Luis Segundo of Uruguay, believe that one cannot separate religion from politics and economics. They teach that the dominated and disenfranchised classes need to dismantle the oppressive systems that keep them powerless. This philosophy and activist perspective could help shift the focus of many of our current intervention programs that serve the oppressed. Rather than merely transferring skills that improve people's ability to adapt to the sociopolitical systems in which they live, these programs could work on changing the oppressive systems themselves.

COMMONALITIES AMONG TRADITIONS

There are important commonalities among these different religious beliefs. For instance, mystical experiences seem to be an integral component of most of these religions. Many religions also refer to energy systems in the body that can be activated for higher states of consciousness and healing. In this country, Wilhelm Reich experimented with healing energy within the body, energy that he called "orgone." Reich believed that this "orgone" was inner energy that could break through the body's armor (Reich, 1948). This energy has been given different names in different cultures. In India it is called *Kundalini* energy, as described by meditating yogis who mapped out the body energy circuits and centers (*chakras*). In China it is called *chi* energy, as discovered by the acupuncturists who traced these energy channels along meridians. In western religions, it has been referred to as the energy of the Holy Spirit. Reich's work with exercises, massage, and deep breathing paved the way for many of the body therapies that are popular in the human potential movement, including bioenergetics, Rolfing, and primal scream therapy. Western medical scientists will one day be better able to identify some of the biological characteristics of these energy states; some have suggested that they are connected to brain peptides and other naturally occurring chemicals influencing the brain.

Many spiritual practices are capable of helping people achieve healthier states of consciousness. It is helpful therefore to focus on common dimensions of these diverse teachings. Anderson and Hopkins (1992) interviewed 30 spiritual women from different religious and spiritual traditions. They were all living the sacred life and were connected to the real essence of their being in their daily activities. Even in despair or crises, they could still see the larger whole, the larger landscape. Often the women experienced a cycling process, alternating between confidence and confusion. However, they always remembered that the path through life was sacred. From these interviews, Anderson and Hopkins concluded that there are multiple paths to the sacred. Many of the women had found the spiritual life after experiencing despair, which helped force them to let go of all mundane certainties in order to gain a larger sense of certainty and determine their true identities. Some of the women followed spiritual practices and others did not, but all were able to see the divine in everyday life.

In Tony Schwartz's book *What Really Matters: Searching for Wisdom in America* (1995), he comes to a similar conclusion: The spiritual path is a process of going forward, slipping, then getting up and trying again. In a sense, the process of being on the path is more important than the ultimate outcome. On this path, both psychological and spiritual practices are necessary, and most people will profit from multiple teachers on this journey to the realization of wisdom.

In the book *Chopping Wood, Carrying Water* (Statser, 1978), Zen masters suggest that we can find spiritual life in everyday life. Compassion and wisdom develop and mature over time, but they rarely emerge with full force. The great wisdom traditions help us identify the wonders that are before us, but it takes time to develop these new ways of seeing the world. The spiritual path is one that sees all of life as a series of opportunities to learn lessons on how to be more loving and kind.

CAUTION IN THE SPIRITUAL APPROACH

The new paradigm that embraces spirituality as a component of psychological health is unpredictable and full of paradox. No doubt there are hidden dangers on the spiritual journey, currently exemplified in the excesses seen in some New Age movements and religions. Many spiritual masters and their practitioners claim exaggerated powers, and many continue to engage in unethical behavior. In the November/December 1990 issue of *Yoga Journal,* Swami Rama, the leader of the prestigious Himalayan Institute, was accused of engaging in sex with his female students (Webster, 1990). Tal Brooke's *Riders of the Cosmic Circuit* (1986) exposed unethical practices that occurred within ashrams of the most respected spiritual gurus. For example, Muktananda allegedly had sexual relations with a number of underage girls. Bhagwan Shree Rajneesh was said to have attempted to break every taboo (including murder, drug smuggling, prostitution, gang rapes, and brutal beatings) as rites of passage. It seems that the danger in spiritual movements—as in other types of movements—is heightened when they have highly visible leaders who accept and use all the power that their followers will give them.

Many spiritual leaders are arrogant and inconsistent in their behavior. Many are rigid and exclusionary in their practices. Enlightenment, they preach, can be achieved only through initiation into their faith. It is not uncommon to find gurus who denigrate religions other than their own. Many of these ideologies are simplistic and narrow in scope. For example, in some of the New Age religions, practitioners say that it is more important to be happy than to be right. This means that they would rather let go of controversy and fail to win others over to their point of view than to persist in argument and experience the psychic and social disturbance that controversy creates. Many who are involved in social change efforts would find this philosophy short-sighted and reactionary. Activists believe that it is more important to be "right" and persevere against difficult obstacles to ensure the success of their causes, even if those efforts result in personal distress and unhappiness.

The core spiritual teachings are relatively straightforward, for they concentrate on cultivating an appreciation of small daily events. Schwartz (1995) maintains that in any field only a small minority of practitioners are committed and effective; there is no reason to assume that this would not also apply to the spiritual domain. There are many highly commercial programs which claim that spirituality can be gained relatively quickly. Such programs must be viewed cautiously. On the spiritual path, the analytic, thinking mind needs to accompany and protect the open heart.

5

A Sense of Community

> The one thing we can be certain about is that in our society the absence or dilution of the psychological sense of community . . . (sense that one was part of a readily available, mutually supportive network of relationships upon which one could depend and as a result of which one did not experience sustained feelings of loneliness) . . . is the most destructive dynamic in the lives of people in our society.
>
> —Seymour Sarason
> *The Psychological Sense of Community*

THE PSYCHOLOGICAL SENSE OF COMMUNITY

Lyon (1989) suggests that a good community fosters public safety, has a strong economy, provides health care and educational opportunities, and has an optimum population size. It is clear that the ecosystem in which one lives has a strong influence on one's ability to develop a balanced and wholesome life. But our ecosystems have been compromised by many factors. Seventy-five percent of Americans now live in cities, and many people experience social isolation in this highly mobile and technological society with its 50 percent divorce rate. People living in the suburbs are no more likely to express satisfaction with their neighborhoods or with the quality of their lives than those living in cities (Adams, 1992). People are looking for relationships that can be characterized as kind and understanding, but it is growing harder and harder to find open and expressive relationships. People's ties with each other are increasingly fragile, and their bonds with others are being disrupted more often as friends move away or change jobs. There is a basic human need to belong, which includes the need for frequent personal contacts and for bonds with others marked by stability and emotional concern (Baumeister & Leary, 1995). Unfortunately, an increasing number of people do not have this bond with others in their lives; these socially isolated people tend to be unhappy.

A possible antidote to this crisis can be found in the development of a psychological sense of community. Sarason (1974) originally defined the term "psychological sense of community" to mean a supportive network, a stable structure that one can depend on for psychological significance and identification. Sarason further stated that the psychological sense of community should be the overarching goal of all community interventions. He (1974) believed that achieving a sense of community is one of the major tasks of life. The absence of this sense of community is one of the most destructive forces in our society, leading to alienation and anonymity.[19]

Part of the attractiveness of mutual support groups, block associations, intentional communities, and voluntary associations lies in their ability to create a sense of purpose and community for their members.[20] Community activism, such as working on public policies and voting, can also help participants develop a sense of community.

A sense of community is positively related to a subjective sense of well-being (Davidson & Cotter, 1989). Moen, Dempster-McClain, and Williams (1989) have found that women who engage in multiple roles and are members of voluntary organizations tend to live longer; more recent research by this group has found that these characteristics also promote psychological well-being. The process of helping others, without regard to outcome, has been found to provide significant health benefits (Luks, 1992).

Characteristics of True Communities

Chertok (personal communication, 7 April 1992) believes that psychological sense of community refers to an organizational feature of a setting, rather than just the individual's experience or a characteristic of the setting. Bishop, Chertok, and Jason (in press) evaluated a scale to measure conceptual constructs in the psychological sense of community. On this scale, Factor 1 is labeled Mission; it encompasses the perception that one is actively engaged with others in the pursuit of a common purpose, which embodies values and goals that transcend individual participants. Formal mission statements, or passages and phrases from materials, may be read and recited at meetings to reinforce the sense of mission. Workshops and presentations that define the setting's mission could be a principal way of attracting new members. Logos, names, and promotional materials can all help define and disseminate the group's mission. Factor 2, labeled Reciprocal Responsibility, refers to the perception that there are acknowledged members of an ongoing group who are mutually responsible to each other. Reciprocal Responsibility connotes that members are seen as valuable resources within the setting, and that the setting responds to the needs of the individuals. This domain concerns the help and assistance people feel they can receive from their fellow group members. People tend to be more satisfied when they believe that all can receive and give something of value. When in a given setting there are more roles than people to fill them, people often feel more welcome to participate.

In some countries, certain regions have a more robust sense of community than others. For example, Putnam (1993) has reported on a 20-year study of social capital (norms of reciprocity and networks of civic engagement) in Italy. Norms of reciprocity include a sense of trust that the benefits one gives to others will be repaid in the future. When communities have more advanced networks of civic engagement, their citizens are more likely to cooperate for the mutual benefit of the community, indicating stronger norms of reciprocity. In northern Italy, there is a substantial stock of social capital, which has led to higher levels of trust, cooperation, and collective well being. In southern Italy, less social capital is in evidence. People show less trust in their neighbors and a greater propensity to use hierarchical solutions, such as coercion and exploitation, in trying to hold society together. These differences in Italian subcultures can be traced back to the eleventh century. At that time in northern Italy, norms of reciprocity and networks of civic engagement were embodied in horizontal civic bonds, such as guilds, mutual-aid societies, cooperatives, and unions, whereas in southern Italy, social and political relations were vertically structured, resulting in mutual distrust, exploitation, isolation, and disorder. If the social context of a region is poor—if people feel exploited and powerless, and if there is little involvement in civic associations—new institutions and reforms will have more difficulty succeeding than in regions with a history of greater social capital.

The Process of Community Building

Peck (1987) suggests that there are four stages of community making. In the first stage, there is pseudo-community, in which people avoid disagreements and just pretend to be a community. During the next stage (chaos), healers attempt to heal and convert others; this is a time of considerable fighting and struggle. During the third stage (emptiness), people begin to remove barriers to communication, such as expectations, prejudice, and ideologies. During the final stage—aptly called community—a peaceful, soft sense of quietude descends. People feel safe to share their vulnerabilities, their sadness, and their joy.

McLaughlin and Davidson (1986) have provided several useful guidelines for building community. First, clear visions, purposes, and common practices need to be established. Attempts to build solid relationships among members are also important. In addition, there must be good processes for resolving conflicts and reaching clear agreements on authority, responsibility, and finances. When qualities of dedication, commitment, positive thinking, flexibility, and ego detachment are cultivated, the probability of developing a successful community is enhanced. Cottrell (1976) has proposed seven conditions that are necessary to enable a community to function competently: enhancing commitment (constituents are willing to work to sustain the community's ability to act effectively); developing a clarity of vision with which different segments of the community can perceive their identities and their interrelationships (constituents can see how the interests of one component are compatible with the interests of other components); fostering the ability of each part of the community to articulate its views, attitudes, and needs; creating procedures to address conflict openly and constructively; maintaining open channels of communication; developing systems for facilitating interaction and decision making; and managing relations with the larger society.

The Natural Community

An apt place to begin our examination of community-building efforts is with communities that have evolved naturally throughout history into cohesive and nurturing environments. There is some evidence that rates of schizophrenia decrease when there are secure and accustomed roles in a community. Murphy (1982, 1983) found low rates of schizophrenia in the Tonga Islands in the South Pacific and in a collectivist pacifist Hutterite sect in western Canada. While excessive individualism and personal insecurity seem to foster schizophrenia, high degrees of social harmony and low degrees of preoccupation with social acceptance and financial security are associated with lower rates of schizophrenia.

An example of a well functioning community is the French Huguenot city Le Chambon. This city is populated by members of a Protestant sect that was persecuted for centuries by the Catholic Church. During World War II, the villagers hid five thousand Jews from the Nazis. Almost all families in the village participated in that humanitarian effort. In this poor rural community, ordinary people performed acts of extraordinary courage, at the risk of their own lives. Without thinking of themselves, they became heroes. In helping others, they were nourished and vitalized. In Lancaster county, Pennsylvania, lives another example of a well functioning community: the Amish. A common norm within the Amish community is the notion that if one is in need, one's brethren will help supply that need. Although they have renounced many modern conveniences, members of this community have a sense of purpose and community that is energizing and meaningful.

BUILDING SUPPORTIVE COMMUNITIES

To attain a psychological sense of community, we should develop traditions, norms, and values that are tied to the settings or communities in which we live. The notion of a supportive community represents a comprehensive way of thinking about health and healing. Such an approach combines strategies that strengthen inner resources by instilling hope, confidence, enthusiasm, and the will to live with strategies that provide a place for people to live that is protected and nourishing.

Many individuals no longer have a strong community or family to provide support, although Etzioni (1993) maintains that many cities have sustained some elements of community and that there are neighborhoods where many people still know their neighbors. Gary Melton (1992) surveyed three inner-city and two small-town communities. When people were asked whom they sought when they had problems with their children, virtually no one mentioned clergy, neighbors, or relatives—sources of help who would have been cited frequently 20 years ago. Instead, the poorer people answered "nobody," or if they cited any source of help, it was the emergency room; whereas wealthier people in suburban areas named professionals from whom they could buy services.

Thousands of individuals are homeless, and others released from state hospitals and detoxification settings have no place to go. Still others live alone and isolated with chronic illnesses or disabilities. Some of our preventive interventions with high-risk children may be compromised or thwarted by the ecosystems in which these children live: The children's vulnerabilities may be directly related to their environment and its inadequate sense of community. For these difficult situations, the psychological sense of community can be an energizing force for problem solving. Community psychologists have many roles to play, including the establishment of supportive settings, collaboration with and advocacy for the creation of such settings, and evaluation of their effectiveness.

The following examples of individuals and groups who have formed alternative settings or communities demonstrate a variety of approaches to individual and community problems (Jason & Kobayashi, 1995). In each of these structured, cohesive settings, members share a common mission, connection, and reciprocal responsibility. These communities were established through the efforts of professionals, ordinary people, and members of disenfranchised groups.

The Lodge

George Fairweather pursued the role of social problem-solving scientist, acting as a research advocate and lobbyist for people with chronic mental illness. Fairweather noted that many patients with mental illness were stable but had little motivation and great institutional dependency. Adaptive behaviors in the hospital did not translate well to the community, and formerly hospitalized patients showed high rates of recidivism (Fairweather, 1979). When chronically mentally ill patients moved back into the community to live, they returned to the hospital at a rate of 70 to 75 percent, irrespective of the types of treatment they had received during hospitalization. Based on these observations and on his experiences with hospitalized individuals, Fairweather voiced the radical notion that people with mental illness could benefit from approaches other than traditional hospitalization and live relatively normal lives in mainstream society. Toward this end a model for community reintegration emerged. It was called The Lodge.

The Lodge was a self-governing organization in which members had participative roles in management and decision making (Fairweather, 1979). Fairweather had previously found that when professionals were present with patients and ex-patients in an organization, the professionals assumed top administrative positions and thus dominated the organization. To avoid this problem, in The Lodge professionals were assigned the roles of consultants, so they could play a meaningful part in the creation of the setting without taking it over. To optimize its chances of success, The Lodge was located in a racially mixed blue-collar neighborhood that was relatively accepting of its existence. As part of the program, members owned and operated their own business, with opportunities for productive work roles. The program was not designed to be transitional but to function as a surrogate family (Tornatzky & Fergus, 1982).

Important evaluation findings over five years included the following: Mutual acceptance and respect of neighbors and Lodge members increased over time; compared to a control group, Lodge members spent a significantly greater amount of time employed and in the community; and the cost of The Lodge was one-third that of traditional community mental health programs. Lodges have now been established throughout the United States. A group called the National Conference of Adopters Coalition for Community Living was established in 1985, to bring all the Lodge adopters together to share ideas for future dissemination of this model program. Fairweather's well-documented experiences provide both precious information for developing new models and an inspiring example of a social scientist committed to the belief that we can participate in the creation of new support systems that enhance the psychological sense of community.

HOME

Like community psychologists, social workers have long advocated the concept that certain problems of individuals, such as social isolation and insufficient social support, can be most effectively addressed through the creation or strengthening of communities. For example, in the late 1800s Jane Addams established Hull House in Chicago to fight the problems faced by poor immigrants struggling to make a new life. Michael and Lilo Salmon provide a contemporary example of this type of commitment and action. They have founded HOME (Housing Opportunities and Maintenance for the Elderly), an organization committed to creating living situations that are supportive and family-like in atmosphere for low-income elders in Chicago. The mission of HOME is to treat elderly people with respect: to preserve their dignity and independence, and to consider them friends rather than clients. Lilo, a social worker, believed that the housing problems of the elderly could be addressed more effectively by creating intergenerational communities. Therefore, the Salmons established intergenerational homes, not as agency programs administered by professionals, but as communities where the staff are also residents or members. In each home live 12 to 14 elderly individuals, a full-time coordinator and his or her family, and several college students who receive free room and board in exchange for completing chores. These intergenerational homes offer elderly residents "an alternative to high rents, loneliness, isolation and the burden of day-to-day self care [and] . . . an innovative communal possibility for a new and different life-style that fosters companionship and friendship by offering the residents the opportunity of caring for each other" (HOME Brochure, 1991, p. 8).

l'Arche

Ordinary citizens have also taken extraordinary steps toward developing communities that offer companionship, friendship, and support in bearing the burden of day-to-day living. In 1964 Jean Vanier, a philosopher, founded l'Arche (the Arch) community, where people with mental retardation and "normal" intelligence live together. Vanier had no formal training in mental retardation; therefore, his approach to people with mental retardation was not affected by the role expectations that human service professionals might bring to such a project. His intention was to create a community built on trust and interdependence. The underlying mission of l'Arche is the creation of a nurturing environment for people with mental retardation (Dunne, 1986). Vanier believed that the barriers that prevent people from making contact must be tackled in the life of each individual through the creation of a more humanizing lifestyle. At l'Arche, community life follows a pattern of work (gardening, housekeeping, or workshop), meals, and recreation. At the heart of the community, members struggle to grow in "their capacity to be more open and loving within the ideals of communitarianism" (Dunne, 1986; p. 47). Dunne further suggests that the sense of community, as experienced in l'Arche, is "an awareness of the relationships and accepting the risks, pain, and weaknesses encountered in self and others" (p. 53). In the years since the project's inception, more than 70 l'Arche communities have been formed.

Needs Foundation

There are other examples of ordinary citizens acting on the realization that the elderly and people with disabilities often need support that is not readily available from the family or society. One such individual is Bill Allison, founder of the Needs Foundation. Bill's wife has multiple sclerosis, and Bill and his wife needed more in-home support than their income and insurance allowed. Bill recognized that his family was not the only one faced with the need for affordable in-home assistance. While watching a television documentary highlighting the plight of the homeless, it occurred to Bill that there were probably homeless people who would be willing to be trained to provide in-home, non-medical care. Such an arrangement would benefit both individuals. The elderly person or the person with a disability would receive affordable assistance, while the caregiver would acquire training, an alternative living arrangement, and work experience. The Needs Foundation facilitates the matching of care receivers and caregivers through an extensive screening and matching process. To date more than a hundred matches have been arranged (Ogintez, 1992). The individuals involved in these relationships find connectedness and a sense of community (Ferrari, Billows, & Jason, 1997).

Oxford House

Individuals demonstrate surprising resilience in creating communities designed to promote their own healing and stability. There are hundreds of Oxford Houses across the country based on the model of the original Oxford House, founded by Paul Molloy and a group of men recovering from alcoholism. Paul Molloy had worked as a Senate committee staff member from 1967 to 1972. During that entire time he had abused alcohol, and in 1975 he left his government position and began his recovery from substance abuse. While living in a halfway house in Montgomery County, Maryland, he saw 12 fellow house members forced to leave the house because they had reached six months' residency, the maximum length of stay. Of these 12 men, 11 relapsed within 30 days. Paul and the other residents then received word that the halfway house had lost its funding and would close within 30 days. After considerable confusion and exchange of ideas with members of the Alcoholics Anonymous (A.A.) community, the residents decided to rent the house themselves. Although they initially had wanted to hire a staff person, they were unable to do so because of the cost. They decided to run the house in a democratic fashion. They named their community Oxford House, after the Oxford Group, an organization that inspired the founders of Alcoholics Anonymous.

In discussing the way the house should operate, local A.A. members urged the residents to keep the house simple. Many had disliked the old halfway house's rules. One house member spoke about his experience in a college fraternity, which had housed 16 men without a house manager. A plan for organizing the house emerged from these discussions. Members agreed that one positive aspect of the halfway house had been its reinforcement of sobriety through the immediate eviction of residents who used alcohol or other drugs. The basic rules of conduct for Oxford House were, and remain, simple: operate democratically, with each member paying his or her rent and doing all assigned chores; and stay sober. Deviation from these rules is cause for immediate eviction. There are no professional staff members at Oxford Houses, and all costs of the program are covered by members.

Six months after the first Oxford House was formed, it had accumulated enough resources to begin a second; members of the second house, in turn, worked to form a third. Within 13 years the number of Oxford Houses had grown to more than 20. In July 1988, Congressman Edward Madigan asked residents of Oxford House for ideas for legislation that would help promote the Oxford House concept nationwide. After residents testified about their experiences, new legislation was introduced to help spread this innovation. A provision within the Federal Anti-Drug Abuse Act of 1988 mandated that each of the 50 states establish a revolving fund of $100,000 to be used to establish group homes for substance abusers along the lines of the Oxford House model. Between 1988 and 1997, the number increased to more than 600 houses. The history of the establishment of the original Oxford House demonstrates the tenacity of a group of people committed to changing their lives.

Oxford Houses for women and children have recently been formed, in response to recovering alcoholic and drug-addicted mothers' need for a safe and sober place to live and raise their children (Dvorchak, Grams, Tate, & Jason, 1995). The houses are affordable places to live, and more stable and secure environments in which to raise children, than shelters, halfway houses, public housing complexes, or the homes of relatives or paramours who still drink and use drugs. Child care is shared by house members, producing a much healthier and more loving environment for the children than they would experience in a drug-abusing environment—or in many of the low-income environments that newly recovering mothers would find affordable—thus reducing their risk of becoming drug abusers in the future. Because residents run the houses themselves and personally affect their environments, Oxford House's democratic system empowers women by allowing them to become more assertive and independent. These supportive fellowships are part of the surrounding community, so women are able to learn about and gain access to local resources and experience a sense of the larger community. These new communities are providing an exciting and powerful opportunity for families who need a second chance—and for researchers studying the process of building community and family.

For the past five years, I have been a member of a DePaul University–based research team that has been involved with the Illinois Oxford Houses in an effort to understand this model (Jason et al., 1994; Jason, Ferrari et al., in press). When I approached the leader of the Oxford House movement, Paul Molloy, he was eager to cooperate with the DePaul University researchers and to receive the benefit of their expertise in program evaluation. Our research team has written proposals for grants to support recruiters who have established new houses. In addition, the researchers have assessed the dynamics and efficacy of the Oxford House model. In April 1994, the *Seattle Times* printed an in-depth article about Oxford House, displaying the success of the houses and reviewing the dynamics behind them (Gelernter, 1994). The DePaul University research team was instrumental in supplying much of the information for the article, which introduces Oxford House to readers in a very positive light, describing the responsible and self-supporting nature of the residences and outlining their struggles and achievements. The team also supplied research findings to defend against a lawsuit filed in the U.S. Supreme Court against an Oxford House in the state of Washington. The suit was based on a zoning law that prohibits more than five unrelated people from living in one dwelling; it was representative of some communities' unwillingness to support Oxford House for fear of reducing their property values. The outcome of this case was positive (the suit against Oxford House was defeated) and it has had a beneficial impact on other Oxford Houses, similar residences, and halfway houses. Community psychologists have important roles to play in helping to evaluate and support these community-building efforts.

Delancey Street Foundation

Delancey Street is a residential self-help center for former substance abusers and offenders. There are more than seven hundred residents in five facilities located in New Mexico, New York, North Carolina, and California. The average resident has been in prison four times. Many are former gang members who have been trapped in poverty for generations. The average resident entering Delancey Street is illiterate and unskilled. Before graduating, residents receive a high school equivalency degree and training in marketable skills. The average stay is four years. In addition to academic and vocational skills, residents learn interpersonal and social survival skills and the sense of responsibility and self-reliance they need to live drug-free in mainstream society. Thousands of men and women have graduated from this program at no cost to the taxpayer, since Delancey Street has no staff and has never accepted any government funds. The entire organization is run by its residents; no salaries are paid, even to the president of the organization. Delancey Street is more like an extended family than a treatment program. Longer-term residents help newer ones, and everyone works. The organization supports itself through its training programs, which provide vocational skills to residents. They include a moving and trucking school, a restaurant and catering service, a print and copy shop, retail and wholesale services, advertising sales, specialty sales, Christmas tree sales and decorating, and an automotive service center.

Delancey Street residents have built a 350,000 square-foot self-managed self-help complex in San Francisco. This four-story complex contains street-level retail stores, a public restaurant, and 177 dwelling units. In addition, it houses educational and recreational facilities that give three hundred formerly unemployed drug addicts and ex-felons training in purchasing, contracting, and computer and accounting services.

Kindness House

In the early 1970s, Bo and Sita Lozoff were living in an ashram in North Carolina. They worked hard on a farm, awoke at four in the morning, ate meals in groups, and refrained from sex. When they visited Bo's brother-in-law in prison, they found that he also worked on a farm, woke up early, ate in groups, and had no sex. While all three were living in similar ways, Bo's brother-in-law hated where he was, while Bo and Sita loved their life. They realized that prisons could be a place where transformative changes could take place. As a result, over time they set up the Human Kindness Foundation.

Bo and Sita began corresponding with prisoners across the country in a project that became known as the Prison-Ashram Project, which now has a mailing list of 20,000 prisoners. They opened Kindness House, which helps prisoners make the transition to the outside world, in May 1994 (Swift, 1995). Residents learn the satisfaction of serving their fellow human beings. They correspond with others and grow their own food. Love and compassion occur more naturally in this setting. Positive attitudes can even be cultivated in prisons, facilitated by people in the community (like Bo, Sita, and their group) who write letters and send books to inmates and conduct workshops in prisons.

Bonaventure House

Adelman and Frey (1994) have described a unique residential facility in Chicago. This setting houses 30 men and women infected with HIV, many of whom already evidence symptoms of AIDS. Founded in 1988 by the Alexian Brothers, a Roman Catholic community of men, Bonaventure House is a vital living community of people with HIV/AIDS. Residents have reported that the opportunity for increased social support was one of their principal reasons for moving into Bonaventure House.

The Alexian Brothers who live in this house are paid a minimum salary and are perceived as figures of great compassion. There is also a paid staff available to help in securing social services and deciphering the rules and forms required for such services. Volunteers offer practical, emotional, and social support.

What distinguishes Bonaventure House from the other communities described in this book is that the residents are living with the reality of death—their own and that of the people with whom they have formed relationships. Group rituals have emerged to deal with the grieving process. For example, there is a balloon-releasing ceremony that functions as a symbolic letting-go of the resident who has died.

Communities encounter a number of problems when they rely on government funds. Many of the residents of Bonaventure House receive government assistance because of their illness, and many are recovering substance abusers. To receive government funding for residents who are recovering from substance abuse, the staff is required to conduct room searches to maintain a drug-free house. This invasion of personal privacy threatens the feeling of community that the staff is trying to foster.

Seaside, Florida

Approximately 13 years ago, Duany and Plater-Dyberk planned a new community in northern Florida (Seaside); since then, they have completed plans for more than 40 additional communities. Seaside was developed to restore a sense of community and an old-fashioned sense of neighborhood. The town's design devalues automobile traffic and frees the streets for people. Porches on each home encourage interaction among residents. In a survey of Seaside residents, Plas and Lewis (1996) found that 72 percent of respondents praised the town's ability to make them feel at home, and 77 percent described having a positive emotional connection with others. In addition, 45 percent spoke of a sense of loyalty to Seaside and its values. The survey's findings included indications that the town's design helped people form emotional connections, the architecture provided opportunities for exchange with neighbors and feelings of membership, and the town philosophy encouraged the development of a sense of community. Finally, 77 percent of interviewees cited the sense-of-community variable as the most important factor that had drawn them to the town. The residents believed that the environmental variables were responsible for the creation of a sense of community.

Other Initiatives

It is not possible to describe all the types of initiatives that people are involved in throughout the country that could fall under the community-building rubric. However, I will briefly mention a few more prominent community-building efforts.

Some Americans are experimenting with co-housing opportunities, a model borrowed from Denmark approximately 23 years ago in an attempt to regain a lost sense of community (Intentional Communities, 1990). Each community member has a private living space; these spaces are arranged around a larger main house, where community activities such as cooking and babysitting occur. Residents have their own kitchens, but at least once a month each resident is required to cook a group meal. These communities tend to include from 12 to 40 households; decisions are made by consensus; and the members work collectively to maintain common areas, such as courtyards and green spaces. This model, which allows for a sense of extended family, could represent the next evolutionary step in housing.

Colleges and universities are also experimenting with new models for developing a sense of community. For example, at DePaul University, The Amate Collegiate House combines community living and volunteerism under one roof. Each student who lives in this residence provides nine hours of volunteer service per week, while living in a community of peers. The volunteers share their experiences and are challenged by discussions on justice, faith, and leadership. Many undergraduates in these settings have become involved in mentoring programs, based on the knowledge that positive mentors have been shown to provide protective influences for at-risk adults and adolescents (Rhodes, Contreras, & Mangelsdorf, 1994).

In Chicago, a neighborhood organization called BUILD has been working for 20 years on developing community-building efforts to discourage adolescents from joining gangs. In a study conducted by Thompson and Jason (1988), school children at risk for joining gangs were provided anti-gang classroom sessions and after-school activities, such as organized sports clinics that encouraged intragroup cooperation. In addition, BUILD staff made it possible for these youth to travel out of their neighborhoods to participate in events and activities with similar groups from other locations. These after-school activities continued throughout the school year. About 10 percent of children from this neighborhood ultimately joined gangs, but none of the youth who participated in this intervention joined a gang. By giving these at-risk children alternative activities and a sense of fellowship and community, BUILD staff were able to protect them from the dangerous gang subculture.

Cowan (1993) has called for the introduction of community-building techniques in workplaces. Managers need to realize that there are alternatives to the ubiquitous use of punishment, shame, and meaningless award programs for motivating workers. Work should be a setting in which one is motivated by care and concern for others. Workers need to be able to express their spirit in their jobs and to speak their minds despite the potential for disapproval. A new attitude and group spirit in work settings could allow workers to be peaceful and calm, bearing witness to both successes and failures without being overwhelmed by doubts or fears.

Religious settings have also been strengthened by community-building efforts. Jason and Lattimore (1990) provide a case example. In an inner-city neighborhood in Chicago, over the past 20 years a Roman Catholic church's membership had changed from Italian to almost exclusively African American. During this period of time, the church services had remained traditional, with the priest assuming the major role and only minimal participation by members. Many of the African-American members of the church had Baptist and Pentecostal religious backgrounds, in which sermons were loud, members actively participated in religious services, and a variety of instruments accompanied the music. Members of the parish noticed that membership and participation in services was gradually decreasing. With the help of a community psychologist, the Liturgy Committee developed a short questionnaire to survey the members and seek ways of increasing the sense of commitment and community. After looking over the returned questionnaires, the committee decided to take steps to increase participation, vigor, and vitality in church activities. For example, at one Mass a children's choir was introduced, and at another Mass an adult choir was formed. After attendance at Masses markedly increased, the church officials began experimenting with other structural changes to promote increased member involvement and ultimately provide a richer source of social support for church members.

Many more examples of this community-building spirit can be cited. Gould Farm provides a secluded retreat and healing milieu for people who need psychiatric treatment and rehabilitation. Grandmother's House, a residential farm in New Mexico, is another example of a community for individuals recovering from serious mental disorders. Grandmother's House offers life- and job-skills training, such as construction classes and job placement. Available work includes gardening, dairy farming, and food production. In 1985, the Mental Patients' Liberation Front, a campaigning group run by ex-patients, opened a user-controlled environment that features self-help, recreational, and advocacy activities. Members are responsible both for making and for enforcing the rules; they thus have a stake in the maintenance of this safe and nurturing environment (Chamberlin, 1996).

A community-building approach is also being used with mentally retarded people at Camphill and Innisfree Village. People First of Illinois, a self-advocacy movement run by and for persons with developmental disabilities, also demonstrates these principles (Miller & Keys, 1996). Wellness communities have been formed in California for people recovering from cancer. The Family Resource Coalition is an advocacy organization working with community-based planning groups to support family self-sufficiency. The Gesundheit Institute is building a health-care community to help people with physical and mental illnesses. In addition, M. Scott Peck has created The Foundation for Community Encouragement, which sponsors community-building weekend workshops (Peck, 1987).

All these communities were built by people with vision and commitment to an ideal. Psychologists, professionals from other disciplines, and ordinary citizens have been involved in the creation of these settings. These types of comprehensive healing environments might exist in many communities, but these settings have rarely been the focus of the work of psychologists and other mental health professionals. I believe that these community-building innovations represent our next frontier.

Comprehensive approaches to community building will one day be more common. There is a clear need for more of these healing places where people's personal journeys can be honored, where helpers and people helped mutually benefit from the process of living together, and where humanitarian and democratic values replace economic issues as the basic goals.

Community-building initiatives need not always involve large groups of people or include housing initiatives. People's efforts on the individual level can help revitalize life settings and lead to a stronger sense of community. For example, a magazine aptly called *Simple Living* has suggested to its readership a number of ways of practicing what it calls simple living. The magazine encourages people to leave their living rooms and gather with others who have similar interests in living simply. At these meetings, people discuss books and articles that help them develop personal strategies for bringing more community and creativity into their lives. They spend time discussing questions such as: How alive do we feel? What forces keep us from experiencing life in depth? What are the things that make us happy? How much of our time is spent in creative activities? How much time do we spend laughing?

Questions for Future Development

Many questions remain unanswered concerning these types of community-building efforts. For example, most of the communities described above have been operated on a rather small scale; it is unclear whether they could be effectively implemented on a larger scale, or whether increased size would encourage the development of power structures, inviting abuses of power. Perhaps instead the proliferation of small-scale projects could lead to a transformation of the larger society.

Many of the communities described above do not emphasize spirituality, but it is possible that those that emphasize common values, traditions, and spiritual paths might have an easier time developing long-term communities. Many of the communities that have been formed are adult-oriented. More communities are needed that focus on children and adolescents. There must be more research to determine the elements that are necessary for community-building efforts to succeed. It is also important to determine appropriate definitions of success for these new communities and to identify potential issues of concern in apparently successful communities. For example, is it possible that some communities are so strong in their adherence to their central doctrines that they are suffocating and unhealthy for the personal development of their members?

Other issues include the best means of disseminating information about successful communities. We also need to determine in which cases it is best to have separate communities for different groups and in which cases it is best to create programs for the general population. Where might funding come from to support these types of initiatives? And on a deeper level, is it possible to transform the current tendency of self-absorption to an external orientation that would support community-building initiatives?

Many would agree that the form and structure of our associations are changing and conclude that sense of community must be found in spite of limited support, by relying on temporary networks and provisional associations. If in fact our society is moving toward an individualistic future, it still is necessary, if not critical, for voices of a different future to be raised. In a sense, our most noble task may be to question our current directions and to provide guideposts for alternative visions, even if those visions may seem impractical for the immediate future.

6

Partnerships with Communities

> When the deepest part of you becomes engaged in what you are doing, when your activities and actions become gratifying and purposeful, when what you do serves both yourself and others, when you do not tire within but seek the sweet satisfaction of your life and your work, you are doing what you were meant to be doing. The personality that is engaged in the work of its soul is buoyant. It is not burdened with negativity. It does not fear. It experiences purposefulness and meaning. It delights in its work and in others. It is fulfilled and fulfilling.
>
> —Gary Zukav
> *The Seat of the Soul*

THE COMMUNITY PSYCHOLOGIST AS PARTNER AND SUPPORT

It is time for further exploration of the practical applications of community psychology. This discipline helps build communities and strengthen community members' capacity to solve their own problems. However, I believe that our efforts would be incomplete—and in some cases potentially dangerous—if they were not undertaken in true partnership with the communities we seek to serve. Community input, community ownership, and community effort are all required if an intervention is to have long-term success. Too many communities have been purely the subjects of interventions, rather than their co-creators. Too often the positive effects of these interventions have faded with the withdrawal of professional attention. A truly effective intervention creates a self-sustaining initiative that will nurture community health and progress long after the intervention is complete. The community psychologist must be available to provide ideas, expertise, resources, and support before, during, and after the intervention.

This chapter provides a series of examples of interventions undertaken in partnerships between community psychologists and community members. Because I know of so many successful interventions worldwide, nationwide (for example, see Biglan, 1995; Fawcett, 1990; Hobfoll, 1988; Winett, 1993), and even in my own city, I have avoided the daunting task of sorting through them by simply choosing the most representative interventions in which I have been involved. I am familiar with these interventions down to the smallest detail, and this option saves me the difficulty of choosing among the work of so many worthy friends and colleagues.

THE COMMUNITARIAN MODEL

Before we look at examples of community-based interventions, let us examine one more contemporary theory of community building. Etzioni (1993) has offered a community model for restoring values and recommitting ourselves to the social fiber of our communities. Etzioni believes that Americans have a strong sense of entitlement but a weak sense of obligation to serve their communities. According to Etzioni and his Communitarian movement, however, there is a core set of values that we can all agree with, and these moral values should be taught in the schools. For example, with rare exceptions, telling the truth is better than lying. Schools need to focus on character formation, and it is easiest to teach self-control when there are clear rules, organizational structure, and guidelines, and assignments are feasible and properly rewarded. Parents have a moral responsibility to invest their time, energy, and other resources in the proper upbringing of their children. Etzioni strongly supports drug-free work sites, environmental protection, and the reduction of bias-related hatred and violence.

While I echo Etzioni's call for greater citizen involvement in the solution of our problems, I must differ with the extent to which he seems to dismiss non-western core values and traditions. While Etzioni states that our overarching values need not be western, he also states that our core values are a commitment to democracy, to the Bill of Rights, and to mutual respect between ethnic and racial groups. And while he admits that a variety of heritages should be embraced, he also states that "those committed to democracy, individual rights, and mutual respect will find little comfort in other major cultural traditions" (Etzioni, 1993; p. 159). Although the Communitarian movement of Etzioni has many constructive elements, this message would alienate many who endorse non-western values and traditions. A variety of cultures have important contributions to make to our core values. In a more inclusive vision of our democratic form of government, credit should be given to some Native American tribes, whose experiments in democracy were known by some of our Founding Fathers. Moreover, our nation could profit from the values of ancient cultures, in which everyday life was honored and people's lives were lived in balance with nature. Western culture has excelled at controlling nature, but we need to study earlier cultures to learn how we can live in harmony with nature.

However, whether we consider our values to be purely democratic or acknowledge the contributions of other cultures, it is essential that we clarify them. Before planning and implementing our interventions, we must ensure that they are in harmony with the values of the communities we serve. If there is such clarity and harmony, our direction will be surer, and our enthusiasm and energy will be less likely to be compromised by inner conflict.

RESEARCH TO ENACT LEGISLATION

The first category of intervention I examine is the use of research to support legislation designed to promote the health and well-being of individuals and communities.

The Pooper-Scooper Caper

My first attempt in this area began with a subject that is neither scholarly nor politically chic: dog litter. The inspiration for the dog-litter intervention came from a Chicago alderman's representative who made a presentation at one of my community psychology classes. I asked the representative what community problem generated the greatest number of resident complaints and personally pledged to work on whatever problem he identified. When the representative uttered the words "uncollected dog feces," my mouth literally fell open in astonishment. In addition to detracting from the aesthetic value of the community, uncollected dog droppings represent a health hazard because they can spread infection and disease.

During the study, researchers observed, for five hours each day on one city block, the number of dogs, the number of dogs who defecated, and the number of dog defecations picked up by dog owners (Jason, Zolik & Matese, 1979). In addition, each morning the researchers collected and weighed all defecations that had not been picked up by dog owners. During the seven-day baseline phase, only 5 percent of dog owners were observed picking up after their dogs, and more than 19 pounds of dog feces were deposited in the target block.

When anti-litter signs were posted during the second phase of the project, relatively few changes occurred on the criterion measures. However, during the next phase, when all dog owners were given instructions and demonstrations on the use of a plastic bag to pick up dog feces, 82 percent of owners picked up after their dogs. These findings indicate that the prompting intervention, which applied both instructions and modeling, effectively motivated dog owners to dispose of their dogs' wastes properly. A 25-month follow-up indicated that there was an 89 percent reduction in dog litter at the intervention site.

A Chicago alderman asked me to present the study results at City Hall, in support of a proposed ordinance that would require dog owners to have pooper-scoopers in their possession when they walked their dogs. This ordinance was passed by the City Council, making Chicago the first city in the country to pass a pooper-scooper ordinance. Many other cities soon adopted similar ordinances. The alderman to whom I had originally provided the data mentioned to me that my study, which received considerable media exposure, had helped change the politicians' perception of this problem, which they had previously considered trivial. The alderman also told me that, because I had been willing to study this issue and document the extent of the problem, legislators were willing—for the first time—to seriously consider enacting legislation to help alleviate the dog litter problem. Later, our team worked with community organizations in Chicago to help them implement campaigns to rid their neighborhoods of uncollected dog droppings (Jason & Zolik, 1985).

The Illinois Child Passenger Restraint Law

Another example of this type of work—on a far more serious topic—is a study I undertook with a colleague in collaboration with the Child Passenger Restraint Association (Jason & Rose, 1984). Each year thousands of children are injured or killed in motor vehicle accidents. In fact, for children under age one, it is one of the leading causes of death. The majority of these injuries and fatalities could be prevented if appropriate child restraints were used. Legislation mandating the use of such restraints represents a viable strategy for dealing with this pressing social problem. Our study evaluated the results of sending technical information to Illinois state senators prior to a vote on a Child Passenger Restraint Bill. We wrote a letter to the senators, which provided them with data supporting the Child Passenger Restraint Bill: Between 1975 and 1981, 140 children in Illinois were killed and 25,828 were injured in automobile accidents; during a nine-month period, an estimated 93 percent of Illinois children were not placed in appropriate restraints when they rode in automobiles; and, in a citizen survey, 78 percent of adults questioned responded that they supported passage of the Child Passenger Restraint Bill. The majority of senators receiving the letter voted for passage of the bill.

On July 1, 1983, the Illinois Child Passenger Restraint Law went into effect. Any child under age four is now required to be secured in an approved child restraint system while riding in a vehicle, and any child between the ages of four and six is required to be placed in either an approved child restraint system or a seat belt. As a result of the law, it is estimated that infant use of appropriate restraints has increased from 49 to 74 percent, and for children aged one to four years, that use of these restraints has increased from 13 to 42 percent. After the law went into effect, deaths of children in Illinois due to traffic accidents over a two-year period decreased by 53 percent (Fawcett, Seekins, & Jason, 1987).

MEDIA-BASED HEALTH-PROMOTION EFFORTS

A practical example of the productive use of technology, media-based health-promotion interventions have the potential to reach large segments of the population. About 15 years ago, I became interested in proactively working with the media by exploring ways of altering inappropriate advertising (Jason & Klich, 1982) and decreasing excessive television viewing (Jason, 1985). These early experiences gave me a conceptual foundation upon which to design and launch a series of large-scale, community-based preventive media interventions. Eight are described below.

Smoking-Cessation Interventions

In 1980 I was asked to serve on the Smoking and Health Committee of the Chicago Lung Association. The committee chairperson had known of my development of school-based smoking prevention programs (Jason, 1979) and my evaluations of methods for establishing non-smoking sections (Jason & Savio, 1978). After serving on this committee for several years, Larry Gruder and I proposed a new direction for the association's smoking cessation initiatives. We recommended to John Kirkwood, the Executive Director of the Chicago Lung Association, that an appropriate goal for 1984 would be to launch a media-based initiative that would reduce barriers to participation in association-sponsored smoking cessation clinics, which had only been attractinog a small group of smokers. Donna Stein, Marketing Director of The Prudential Insurance Company's health maintenance organization (PruCare HMO), generously agreed to underwrite a large-scale smoking cessation program.

During January 1985, we worked with Channel 5, the NBC affiliate in Chicago, on adapting the American Lung Association's self-help program, "Freedom From Smoking in 20 Days," for presentation on the evening news. The series was broadcast on Channel 5's 4:30 P.M. and 10:00 P.M. news broadcasts. Approximately 500,000 viewers watched the 10:00 P.M. broadcast. Fifty thousand self-help manuals, which represented a step-by-step procedure for gradually reducing smoking and ultimately quitting, were distributed in more than 300 True Value Hardware stores.

There were 431 companies who participated in the program by getting manuals. The Chicago Lung Association conducted twice-weekly support group meetings at 21 work sites during the three-week program. Forty-one percent of those who attended the group meetings were abstinent by the end of the program, but only 21 percent of non-attendees, who were provided with self-help manuals and watched the television broadcasts, had quit (Jason et al., 1987). At a one-year follow-up, the abstinence rate was the same (21 percent) for those provided group meetings, media intervention, and manuals and those who just received the media intervention and manuals (Jason et al., 1987). A reasonable conclusion is that brief group interventions must be followed by ongoing support and reinforcement. This large-scale project was developed and implemented without state or federal funds. A number of voluntary associations, community groups, and for-profit corporations worked eagerly on this project and donated resources because each group reaped enormous publicity gains from its sponsorship of this popular community intervention.

This successful first effort completed, we sponsored another smoking cessation program in November 1985, again with PruCare HMO and the Chicago Lung Association. During this second project, WGN-Channel 9—a superstation whose programming is beamed via satellite throughout the United States and Central America—carried the 20-day program. For this program, 100,000 manuals were distributed through True Value Hardware stores (Jason, Tait, Goodman, Buckenberger & Gruder, 1988). Nielsen ratings conducted during the month in which the health promotion program was aired indicated that approximately 286,000 and 583,000 people in the Chicago area watched the 12:00 noon and 9:00 P.M. broadcasts of the program, respectively. Epidemiological data suggest that approximately one-third of these viewers were likely to be smokers.

The January and November 1985 interventions reached an estimated 150,000 smokers; if only 10 percent (a very conservative estimate) achieved long-term abstinence, then our programs helped 15,000 people quit smoking. The public health implications of these findings are important in that the lifetime health savings from the prevention of chronic diseases (such as cancer) for each middle-aged adult who quits smoking is conservatively estimated to be $40,000. If 15,000 people stopped smoking, this would create an estimated $600,000,000 in health-care cost savings (Oster et al., 1984). In other words, these two health promotion programs, which relied solely on resources from the local community, potentially saved hundreds of millions of dollars. This does not even begin to assess the value of the prolongation of individual lives.

In spring 1987, Brian Flay and other researchers, including myself, received federal funds to mount a third televised smoking cessation intervention, which was broadcast for 20 days on the local Chicago ABC television station. Because in the first study we found that many participants in the group meetings who had stopped smoking by the end of the program relapsed later (Jason et al., 1987), for this study DePaul University researchers conducted 12 monthly follow-up support groups and provided incentives in the form of a lottery for participants at work sites throughout the Chicago metropolitan area (Jason et al., 1989). At a 24-month follow-up, the rate of abstinence for participants who attended the group meetings, watched the media presentation, and received manuals was significantly higher than the rate for those who only watched the media presentation and received manuals (30 percent compared to 19 percent) (Salina et al., 1994). These results indicate that follow-up groups and incentives helped reduce the erosion effects that frequently occur at the completion of smoking cessation interventions. The media can be used to reach thousands of people and to prepare them for health promotion intervention. Support groups can then reinforce the messages from the media and self-help materials and provide the structure, reinforcement, and encouragement to make behavior changes (see Jason, McMahon et al., 1995).

Smoking Prevention in African-American Communities

In November 1989, a comprehensive prevention program was implemented to decrease the incidence of new smokers within the African-American adolescent population in Chicago. This program combined a school-based curriculum with a comprehensive media intervention (Kaufman, Jason, Sawlski, & Halpert, 1994). The Board of Education supplied 472 elementary schools in Chicago with copies of "Smoking Deserves a Smart Answer," a curriculum developed by the American Lung Association.

The curriculum was introduced into the schools in conjunction with the launching of a media intervention, which was divided into three components. The first component was implemented through *The Chicago Defender*, a Chicago-based newspaper with a daily circulation of 30,000 to predominantly African-American readers. Publishers of *The Chicago Defender* agreed to print a smoking prevention curriculum on their weekly children's page.

The second component of the media intervention was disseminated through WGCI, a Chicago-based radio station with a predominantly African-American listening audience of more than one million people. WGCI ran eight smoking prevention public service announcements during October and November 1989. In addition, WGCI aired a call-in talk show with a focus on helping parents improve communications with their children, thereby empowering parents to help their children combat environmental factors influencing them to smoke. WGCI also promoted and aired the winning entries of a Smoking Prevention Rap Contest for school children. The entries were required to convey a message encouraging their peers not to start smoking cigarettes. Winners were chosen from five different age groups. Grand prize winners from all age groups had their raps aired on WGCI's Friday Night Rap Show; the overall winner was a guest DJ on that show.

In the third component of the media intervention, Gannett Outdoors, the owners of approximately two-hundred billboards in the Chicago area, sponsored a smoking prevention poster contest. As with the rap contest, the children learned about this competition through announcements in all Chicago public schools. The rules of the contest required children to develop posters conveying messages designed to discourage others from starting to smoke. A winner was chosen from each of five age groups, and Gannett turned each of the winning posters into a billboard displayed in five different locations in the Chicago area. In addition to receiving individual prizes, each of the winners was presented with a certificate and a prize for his or her school at a special assembly.

The results of this intervention are encouraging: Students decreased their use of tobacco and reported lower family use of cigarettes, alcohol, and marijuana. My colleagues and I believe these favorable effects are a product of the community-wide, comprehensive nature of the intervention. They demonstrate the success that we may achieve through partnership between researchers and community members. The reports of decreased family substance use indicate that parents' habits changed after they became involved with their children's homework assignments. In fact, many parents participated in the radio and newspaper components, to the extent that they listened to WGCI's call-in show and read *The Chicago Defender*'s anti-smoking messages. These results also support the hypothesis that family involvement is effective in implementing substance abuse interventions.

Also vital to the success of the project were the relationships among the researchers and the Chicago Lung Association, community organizations, schools, and the media. All were true collaborators and participants in this project. These partnerships seem especially important when one considers that the target population was urban African-American children, rather than the more common target population of white middle-class suburbanites. The WGCI rap contest is a good example of effective cultural awareness. The intervention made use of a preexisting, common, and enjoyable activity of urban African-American children, in order to motivate their interest and make learning fun. The students were able to use their own language and style, thus making the antismoking message meaningful and memorable.

Drug Abuse Prevention

Our next study was of a statewide substance-abuse prevention program, Kids InTouch, targeted at children and parents, which was initiated by the Illinois Department of Alcohol and Substance Abuse in spring 1990 (Jason, Pokorny, Lahmar, & Bennetto, 1994). The first component of this intervention was an "In Touch" supplement in the *Chicago Tribune,* which was distributed prior to the telecast of a daily series of news segments. Circulation on the day of distribution was 1.2 million copies. The *Tribune* supplement provided a daily format that coincided with the upcoming news series. In addition, the supplement included family exercises and anti-drug drawings and messages by students. The supplement contained a statewide resource guide to substance abuse prevention activities and other supportive services, state and national referral services, and a phone number for parent training workshop sites.

A daily series on WGN television was aired on the 12:00 noon and 9:00 P.M. news. The purpose of the WGN television component was to build awareness, increase sensitivity to issues of substance abuse, and announce parent training groups throughout Illinois. The six-part news series combined facts about drug initiation, substance abuse, and children of parents dependent on alcohol and other drugs. Special interest profiles of Chicago families who had addressed these issues were also included. Information about parent training workshops was given at the close of each news segment.

Approximately six hundred human service agency staff and community workers were trained to conduct the parent training workshops, which were open to all residents of Illinois. In comparison to a control group of parents, those participating in the parent training workshops showed significant improvement in alcohol and other drug knowledge and in parenting skills.

Another component of this multilevel intervention was the "High Top Tower" series, which aired Saturday mornings on Chicago's Channel 32 for six consecutive weeks, beginning on November 10, 1990. Other stations across the state aired the program on different days and in a variety of time slots. Since the series was intended to reach children prior to drug initiation, the content of the weekly broadcasts addressed such issues as self-esteem, tactics for resisting use, problem solving, and alternatives to drugs.

The final program component was a school-based curriculum that consisted of 12 classroom activities designed for children ages 5 to 12. Like the "High Top Tower" television series, it covered such topics as self-esteem, family structure, health and safety, and information about alcohol and drugs. The school-based curriculum became available to school teachers across the state in the winter of the 1990–91 school year. Statewide, 2,137 copies of the curriculum were distributed.

Stress-Management Intervention

During spring 1986, WGN television joined the Chicago Lung Association, PruCare Health Maintenance Organization, and True Value Hardware stores in producing a stress management program (Jason, Curran, Goodman, & Smith, 1989). The program was aired daily on the 12:00 noon and 9:00 P.M. WGN news. At True Value Hardware stores in the Chicago area, 170,000 free manuals entitled "Success Over Stress" were distributed to the public. The manuals were designed to help viewers follow the daily TV broadcasts and to provide supplementary exercises and activities. The daily broadcasts featured the following components: defining stress, describing the body's response to stressors, identifying major life stressors, assessing one's social support network, and identifying a variety of behavioral, cognitive, and psychological coping strategies for dealing with stress.

This primary preventive program was developed and funded by local sponsors, which received valuable publicity as a result. The television program on stress management was so popular it was aired during "sweeps week," a time when television stations closely monitor their audiences.

Nutrition and Weight Reduction Intervention

During a three-week period in fall 1986, another large-scale health promotion program cosponsored by the Chicago Lung Association was launched on WGN. This series featured daily reports on the 12:00 noon and 9:00 P.M. news concerning healthy nutritional practices and effective exercises (Jason, Greiner, Naylor, Johnson, & Van Egeren, 1991). In addition to this media component, the intervention included the distribution of 100,000 self-help manuals on the series throughout Chicago at True Value Hardware stores. As in the stress reduction program, all resources were generated from the local community. One component of this overall study involved a group of viewers who had weight problems. A randomly selected group attended ongoing weight-control self-help groups, watched the television show, and read the self-help manuals. This group succeeded in losing more weight than a comparable group, which was only exposed to the media program and manuals and did not attend meetings.

HIV/AIDS Prevention in Families

"Families InTouch: Understanding AIDS," which was partially funded by the Centers for Disease Control, was a multimedia health promotion strategy targeted toward HIV/AIDS prevention within the family unit (Crawford et al., 1990). In fall 1988, for six consecutive days, five- to ten-minute segments on AIDS and the family were televised on the 12:00 noon and 9:00 P.M. news broadcasts on WGN. In addition, a 16-page supplement appeared in the Sunday *Chicago Tribune*. On the Sunday before the telecast, 1,200,000 copies of the *Chicago Tribune* were distributed. "Families InTouch" provided factual information about AIDS, including means of transmission and prevention. It focused on improving the family's effectiveness in educating its members about the dangers of drug abuse and high-risk sexual practices by providing information relevant to the family and interactive exercises for parents and children designed to enhance communication, problem solving, decision making, and values clarification. The exercises were included in the *Chicago Tribune* AIDS Prevention Supplement. The "Families in Touch: Understanding AIDS" program represented a departure from most other AIDS prevention programs in its attempt to incorporate the use of the media as an intervention strategy and the targeting of the family as the unit of change. Children who watched the program spoke more about sexual issues within their families and became more knowledgeable about AIDS.

FORMING COMMUNITY ALLIANCES

There are abundant opportunities to find local resources to develop and implement these types of large-scale preventive and health-promotion interventions. However, the success of this approach depends on associating and working with networks of supportive grassroots organizations. Early on I developed a relationship with the Chicago Lung Association's Smoking and Health Committee. This organization provided entry into a number of other critical organizations. When the committee set as a priority the launching of a media-based smoking cessation intervention, we were fortunate that a progressive HMO was simultaneously seeking to launch a similar project. Once these alliances were formed, we gained access to a number of television stations and other businesses. After the success of our first program, we had easy entry into other television stations and organizations.

Key factors in our success were patience and readiness to use a vast set of networks, each of which gained direct, tangible benefits from their participation. For a number of these interventions, the Chicago Lung Association and PruCare Health Maintenance Organization provided staff to develop the programs and funds to print the manuals, in exchange for considerable media coverage. Approximately two-hundred 15- and 30-second promotions aired prior to many of the interventions, and the primary sponsors were identified in each promotion. True Value Hardware also provided financial resources in exchange for publicity on television, association with a worthy public health effort, and potential customers coming into their stores to pick up manuals. Each of the sponsors had its organization's name printed prominently on the self-help manuals and promotional materials. The television stations were identified with a credible community-based health promotion program, which helped to attract new viewers.

The media represents an excellent forum to alert thousands of community residents to health-promotion initiatives. Once alerted to these programs, participants can pick up materials and resources that reinforce the concepts broadcast and encourage opportunities for practice. Perhaps the most exciting possibilities lie in more interactive interventions. Groups can be assembled to watch the programs together; or participants can receive additional support by being put in touch with helpers, self-help groups, or other community agencies. Many efforts to alter addictive behaviors have been unsuccessful in producing long-term change. Perhaps by lowering barriers to participation in programs, and by devising imaginative ways to enable participants to continue receiving support and encouragement following the end of the media programs, we will be able to engender sustained improvement.

7

Wisdom Traditions as Our Guide

What more chilling commentary on the modern world could there be than that most people die unprepared for death, as they lived, unprepared for life.

—Sogyal Rinpoche
The Tibetan Book of Living and Dying

BREAKDOWN AND TRANSFORMATION

There is considerable evidence that we are witnessing a breakdown in the psychological sense of community. Putnam (1995) has documented dramatic decreases in the number of organizations that involve civic participation, such as the Elks, the League of Women Voters, and bowling leagues. More people are participating in solitary activities, using widespread technologies such as TVs, VCRs, and stereos. Constant restructuring within American corporations has resulted in unprecedented profits for shareholders, but hundreds of thousands of American workers have lost their jobs (Dugger, 1995). People in third-world countries aspire to America's economic development ideology because they see its materialistic lifestyle as an antidote to their poverty. Whether one looks at rates of divorce, homelessness, or crime, there are severe problems facing our society, and at least some of it can be blamed on the individualistic preoccupations of contemporary citizens of industrialized countries. In chapter 2, I argued that a cluster of vulnerabilities has converged during this century to separate us from our past ancestry, our vital symbols, and our roles and communities.

ROLES OF THE COMMUNITY PSYCHOLOGIST

The field of community psychology emerged in the late 1960s. It represented an effort by some psychologists to become more active in helping to solve some of the social and community problems that confronted our country during that turbulent period. Duffy and Wong (1996) recently described the characteristics that distinguish this branch of psychology: emphasis on prevention rather than treatment and on strengths and competencies rather than weaknesses; an ecological perspective that examines the relationships between people and their environment; appreciation and respect for diversity and differences; stress on empowerment, which involves enhancing the processes by which people gain control over their lives; emphasis on action research and social change, which provide more alternatives; collaboration with other disciplines; and reliance on interventions that build a sense of community.

In the field of community psychology, there have been several approaches proposed to help deal with this country's enormous social problems. For example, generic primary preventive strategies include modifying the environment by such methods as increasing social support or decreasing the effects of stress; eliminating stressful agents by such methods as legislative initiatives or psychological interventions; and strengthening the competence of the host to deal with stressors (Gesten & Jason, 1987).

Cook and Shadish (1986) have suggested that there are three ways of implementing social change. The most successful model involves making incremental modifications in existing social programs. Few policies are approved if they call for more than marginal changes in the status quo. A bolder approach is the use of demonstration programs to test the efficacy of a planned innovation; however, many successful demonstration programs have never been widely replicated. On the other end of the spectrum lie the interventions that change basic social structures, but these types of changes are rare. Albee (1986), a supporter of this model, believes that we will always have undesirable levels of psychopathology as long as we have exploitation; imperialism; excessive concentration of economic power and nationalism; and institutions that perpetuate powerlessness, poverty, discrimination, sexism, racism, and ageism. Although the elimination of these conditions is a laudable goal, this book argues that only a transformation of our values will provide sufficient motivation and willingness to work on the forces that cause unequal distribution of the world's resources.

Many advocates of community psychology have adopted a competence-building approach that involves systematically teaching clusters of personal or social skills to promote competence or prevent psychological dysfunction. An alternative model focuses on empowerment, which involves strategies to enhance justice and people's sense of control over their own destinies (Rappaport, 1981).

The paradigm that has captured the attention of many community psychologists is the ecological model (Mann, 1978). Lewin's (1951) seminal work emphasized the interdependence of the person and the environment in determining behavior, and Barker (1968) continued this work with his emphasis on non-psychological behavior. Moos (1984) and Sarason, Carroll, Maton, Cohen, and Lorentz (1977) have continued to elaborate upon the ecological approach. Kelly and his colleagues, particularly Ed Trickett, are some of the leading theorists in this fascinating line of research (Kelly, 1977, 1985, 1987, 1990; Trickett, Kelly, & Vincent, 1985). Kelly's goal has been to develop theories of how people become effective and adaptive in varied social environments. The ecological paradigm is a guiding framework for understanding behavior in interaction with its social and cultural contexts.[21]

Kingry-Westergaard and Kelly (1990) have recently suggested that a fundamental principle of ecological approaches is the need to use multiple methods to understand the complex qualities of relationships and systems. An important method used in the ecological approach is to increase our understanding of what we claim to know through a collaborative relationship: Concepts and hypotheses are developed and tested by both researcher and participants. The ecological endeavor is a discovery process in which researcher and participants share the different constructions of their contexts, learn about events and processes that help define their understanding of these contexts, and work together to define the research activity.

Much of the attention of community theorists has been directed to the skills and abilities that children and adolescents need, as well as, to a somewhat lesser degree, the opportunities they have to display such competencies and be rewarded for engaging in positive behavior. Unfortunately, the ecological context does not always receive the attention it deserves. We regularly see youngsters with clear social skill deficits. In observing their difficulties we are motivated to find ways of being helpful—often through assessment and intervention. This desire to do something can at times prevent us from understanding the macro-level forces that have produced the social incompetence; without attention to these systemic variables, our efforts are likely to be less comprehensive and less effective.

Operation Snowball

There are many excellent school-based drug abuse prevention programs that operate on the premise that certain skills and abilities can be taught and that youngsters who have learned effective life skills will be more resistant to using drugs. These programs focus on the individual student. Family bonding is sometimes considered in these programs; however, the number of studies that take this factor into consideration is exceedingly small.

As an alternative, schools and communities—as partners—can assess norms within the schools and begin changing the standards for acceptability. Operation Snowball in Illinois is an example of one such program. Youngsters and adult role models spend time together developing school programming that extends beyond one classroom or one series of lessons on drug abuse and emphasizes constructive messages, values, and beliefs. When participants actively set up alternative drug-free settings such as dances and fundraisers, the drug-free ideology is woven into adolescent notions of what is appropriate. In addition, when youngsters take on the task of helping others, the system slowly begins to change. The helping roles represent a countercultural movement, launched into a subculture that formerly endorsed inappropriate risk-taking behaviors.

Also possible is a more radical approach, one that views the school within its larger context. The values of our society directly affect the ways in which children make decisions about a variety of health-enhancing and health-compromising behaviors. For example, if society allows children easy access to dangerous substances, then we are sending a clear message of permission to our youth. If our competency-enhancing programs are situated within environments that openly contradict these programs' primary messages, their effectiveness will be limited.

The Woodridge Project: A System-Wide Intervention

Let me be more specific and provide an illustration of a system-wide intervention. For a number of years I have been interested in developing strategies to decrease the incidence of smoking by children, of whom an estimated four thousand begin the habit each day (Rhodes & Jason, 1988). In 1988, I switched my attention to the merchants and store owners who sell cigarettes to minors even though this transaction is against the law. When our community's merchants openly sell cigarettes to minors, they are sending the insidious message that it is acceptable for children to be smoking. Giving children easy access to cigarettes is reprehensible, since smoking accounts for more than a quarter of a million deaths in this country annually (Rhodes & Jason, 1988). In my study, I found that about 80 percent of the stores in the Chicago area that sold cigarettes sold them to minors. These findings were extensively publicized by the media in the Chicago area (Jason, Ji, Anes, & Xaverious, 1992). The state law prohibiting such sales was not effective because a police officer first would have to observe a minor purchasing cigarettes and then take the store owner to the police station to process the complaint. A criminal trial could then take place—a time-consuming process for the police officer. It is not surprising that police officers rarely arrested merchants for this offense.

Officer Talbot of Woodridge, a suburb of Chicago, contacted me after my study had been publicized. He said that the Chief of Police had addressed this problem in his community by sending a letter to all merchants explaining the Illinois law prohibiting cigarette sales to minors under 18. I told Officer Talbot that, based on my experience, this letter would probably not change the merchants' behavior. We decided to work together to investigate the problem and its possible solutions. Over the next two years, we sent several minors on a regular basis into all the community's stores to assess the extent to which cigarettes were sold to minors. In August 1988, 70 percent of the community's stores sold cigarettes to minors. At this point, we began developing legislation to attack this problem. In November 1988, the sales rate was 60 percent. In February 1989, the sales rate was 79 percent.

Working with these data, Officer Talbot and I helped draft Woodridge's Tobacco Licensing and Enforcement Law, which was passed on May 1, 1989. The law required merchants to buy a license to sell cigarettes. This feature of the law had several benefits. First, the money could be used to repeatedly monitor compliance with the law. Second, the first time store owners violated the law, they were warned; the second time, their license was suspended, causing them a significant loss of income. The law required all vending machines to be outfitted with a special lock, which could be opened only by an employee. Therefore, minors no longer had open access to cigarette machines. If store employees sold cigarettes to minors, they would be ticketed. In addition, although state law allowed this practice, merchants could not rely on a note from a parent saying the purchase was for an adult according to the city law.

In June 1989, soon after passage of the law, we found that 33 percent of stores sold cigarettes to minors. First offense warnings were issued to these stores. The remaining stores that refused to sell cigarettes to minors received letters from the police thanking them for their compliance. We sampled again in August 1989, and 36 percent of the stores sold to minors; half were repeat offenders from June. The repeat offenders received a one-day cigarette license suspension and a $400 fine. No merchant contested the penalty. In November 1989, and January 1990, we repeated our study. None of the stores sold to minors.

The significant finding is that we found less than 5 percent of merchants sold cigarettes to minors in Woodridge for over a year after passage and enforcement of the sales enforcement and vendor licensing provisions. Presampling education and awareness efforts (in the form of the police department's informative letter) were ineffective. Woodridge is the first community in the nation to document sustained reductions in illegal cigarette sales to minors as a result of legislation and enforcement (Jason, Ji, Anes, & Birkhead, 1991). During all phases of the study, I met with Officer Talbot and other police personnel to develop each step of this collaborative project. When baseline data indicated high sales levels, that information was used to gain support for the legislation. After passage of the legislation, continued sampling indicated that the problem, although reduced, still existed. These data helped convince our team of the need for continuous monitoring and feedback to the merchants. Most important, two years after passage of this legislation, cigarette smoking among Woodridge youth had been reduced by more than 50 percent (Jason et al., 1991). In other words, when access to cigarettes grew more difficult, fewer youths began experimenting with them.

In 1996 we conducted another follow-up investigation and found significantly less cigarette smoking in Woodridge and another community with similar laws, compared to communities without such laws. In addition, in Woodridge there was significantly less marijuana use as well. In towns with enforcement, the adolescents said that over the past year they had been approached less frequently by someone trying to give or sell them illegal drugs (Jason, Berk, Schnopp-Wyatt, & Talbot, 1997).

Since passage of the legislation, we have been approached by dozens of surrounding communities interested in initiating similar campaigns. In addition, congressional hearings concerning cigarette sales to minors were held in 1990, and Officer Talbot presented our study at these hearings. In spring 1990, Health and Human Services Secretary Sullivan proposed a national legislative initiative to reduce cigarette sales to minors. Many of the major features of this proposed legislation were adopted from the Woodridge study. In 1992 the Synar Amendment was passed, and our work in Woodridge was used as a model that states around the country could follow in solving this problem. In addition, Officer Talbot became a national authority on this topic and has continued to consult with federal organizations and cities throughout the United States on ways of helping them reduce illegal sales of cigarettes to minors.

THE ECO-TRANSFORMATIONAL MODEL

I have coined the term ecological transformational, or eco–transformational, to describe the types of work described in this book. I believe that community psychologists function as visionaries and mystics by identifying the issues that we as a society will need to face and deal with in the future. Community psychologists also engage in archeological excavations to better understand the historical, philosophical, and epistemological issues that contribute to our current social problems. The field of community psychology is predicated on the assumption that some of our most complex and intransigent social and community problems can be synergistically transformed by the recognition, appreciation, and utilization of the assets and inner resources that already exist within social settings. This function represents the alchemist role of the community psychologist. And finally, the discipline espouses a commitment to public articulation of our values; by such action, we explicitly adopt the distinct role of advocate, while many other social scientists adopt more impartial program evaluation roles.

Two questions central to any intervention—and to intervention processes as a whole—are whether there are fundamental developmental and psychological initiations that we as human beings need to progress through, and whether certain core values may underlie our efforts to help others. Without road maps or guides, it may be difficult to design interventions that address the structural issues that create so much isolation and alienation. To the extent that we are dealing with a crisis of values and a breakdown in the psychological sense of community, our methods of conceptualizing our problems may require historical and philosophical theories as anchor points for deeper analysis.

In more primitive times, there were rituals, customs, and rites that helped ease the transition from the dependent status of youth to the more independent role of adulthood. Some of the problems of our youth may represent an attempt to deal with the loss of the myths and rituals that gave previous generations a more tangible sense of meaning within society. Some of our efforts could be used to explore the remnants of ancient mythologies that still exist within our youth and to actively help them recreate myths that are meaningful to their families and communities.

Many of our social interventions and conceptualizations of community problems have omitted reference to heuristic ideas within the fields of history, philosophy, and mythology. Some social scientists consider such ideas to be incompatible with the scientific method. However, it can be argued that a broadened conceptualization yields many benefits. For example, each individual life has its psychological and metaphysical themes, and their resolution greatly influences the ability to participate in a communal or family setting. Because each person is on his or her own unique voyage and has different shadows to contend with, it is not unusual for conflict to occur among those who are trying to create new collective settings. Although each journey is a solo mission, a critical task along that journey is to learn to live together in community. This is an element often neglected by those describing the spiritual journey: the creation of social settings that provide a sense of community to all members and a sense of meaning to one's spiritual yearnings, and altruism that refuses to be preoccupied with one's own individual needs.

The social competence approach is limited by its ahistorical and philosophical tenets. For example, many interventions within this model can help individuals become more independent and raise their self-esteem; however, this result can reinforce tendencies to become less interconnected with family and community. The ecological perspective does not indicate which groups to collaborate with, and it is apparent that there are many community groups and organizations whose missions are directed toward control and domination of other people and of the environment. As for the empowerment model, again the question arises as to which groups to help empower.

The wisdom traditions could provide guides for energizing the visions of a new paradigm. An eco-transformational model, the term that I use for this new paradigm, suggests that interventions should be sensitive to the vulnerabilities discussed in chapter 2. Eco-transformational interventions help people become aware of their biological urges, the primitive shadows that have both aggressive tendencies and creative and playful parts. Eco-transformational interventions support protective self-regulatory processes that channel these energizing forces into productive cultural outcomes. Eco-transformational programs support our interconnectedness with the natural world and help us live in balance with nature, as opposed to trying to control her. This model supports scientific and technological investigations that help explore the mysteries of life, and reaffirms and validates the importance of rituals, traditions, and initiatory processes that help people and their communities mature and develop intimate bonds. Finally, eco-transformational interventions attempt to recapture the sense of community that provides responsibility, mission, and commitment to the welfare of one's community. The wisdom traditions speak to deep sources within our souls. Our analyses and social programs would be immeasurably enriched by learning how to honor our thoughts (through Buddhist practices), love our bodies (as practiced in the goddess traditions), appreciate the world of nature (as in Native American traditions), care for those in need (based on ethics from the great western religions) (Spretnak, 1991), and develop a robust sense of community.

These foundational values inspire our enthusiasm and commitment to a particular problem; they tap energizing components that sustain long-term involvements with social issues; they center our actions and allow us to persevere despite numerous obstacles; and they establish visionary, transcendent values for a more protected and connected future. Why do people feel so intensely when they listen to music, look at a piece of art, or undergo a religious experience? Why do some people spend countless hours raising funds for causes or devoting their lives to the attainment of an ideal, when there are few monetary incentives for such activities? Foundational values can provide passion, zeal, and commitment. These inward forces sustain and nourish the voyages to often unattainable shores that represent our greatest challenges, our noblest ventures, and our most human activities. If our work touches these generative springs, it will have a better chance of capturing the public's imagination and the decision maker's agenda.

These values form a life-thread of energy, more mysterious than documentable, but tangible nonetheless. We need to learn to see what we can barely hear, to feel what is as omnipresent as the air we breathe, and to smell the colors that pervade our senses. As we begin to live by these values, our analyses will be sharper, our collaborations richer, our missions clearer, and our work more meaningful and ultimately more socially important.

The future will in all probability be a brave new world, with the full spectrum of tendencies: independence and separation on the one hand, interconnectedness and spirituality on the other. It is understandable that, as we emerged from nature, these two ways of being in the world would present our greatest challenge. It is also possible, however, that our efforts to control and dominate through technology will provide the leisure in which we can more fully appreciate and explore the alternative paradigm of interconnectedness and community. Our planet will face many significant problems in the coming years, including the need to feed an escalating population, increased poverty in many countries and excessive waste of resources in others, and environmental degradation. As a society, we need to find ways to focus on improving the quality of life and fulfilling our responsibility to our communities, rather than on increasing profits and economic development.

Two billion years ago, the first bacteria that developed were solely exploitive, but over time they learned to become cooperative (Sahtoris, 1989). Our systems and our lives are far more complicated than those of bacteria, and so our transformational processes are undoubtedly more complicated than theirs. However, given the traditions and values that lift us above the limits of our animal nature, we cannot say how much farther we may evolve and what benefits may befall the whole of humankind.

Afterword: An Eco-Transformational Application: Bridging the Macro to the Micro

As a social worker and trauma specialist who treats people with disabilities and chronic illnesses, including Post Traumatic Stress Disorder (PTSD), Lupus, and Chronic Fatigue Syndrome, I have long been aware of the ongoing necessity to provide interventions that consider the context and culture of the identified patient as well as that of the healthcare professional. Treatment approaches that ignore the ecological exchange between patient and provider typically are limited in their effectiveness and can in fact be damaging and even traumatizing to the patient and his or her family and community. The long social work tradition of assisting the individual through strengthening the living environment and helping to create community, echoed throughout Jason's volume, is unquestionably critical.

The eco-transformational approach put forth in his work considers sociocultural influences as well as the individual as part of a multi-layered social exchange system. It also clearly values the need to include other systems of knowing—philosophy, mythology, history—beyond the mechanistic, linear and behavioral scientific approaches typically applied to understanding and treating social issues.

I have seen sociocultural influences converge within the cultural framework of our society and create a social context and discourse, which dictates social beliefs and values such as social attitudes toward social problems, disability, illness and treatment; and social roles played between patients and practitioners, and patients and their communities. These influences create a social discourse within which a social issue, disease entity, or syndrome is recognized or "born," investigated, treated, and ultimately enculturated. Subsequently, a history emerges within a social framework, which includes families and communities as primary actors. Within this framework, persons encounter beliefs and attitudes that are sometimes stigmatizing and traumatizing.

Specific factors of this social framework need to be carefully considered in the assessment and treatment of individuals, families, and communities. Within the context of community, the most prominent factors include (1) cultural intolerance of suffering; (2) cultural intolerance of ambiguity; (3) cultural intolerance of chronic as opposed to acute social issues; (4) the ongoing psyche-soma duality among care providers; and (5) initial social issue illegitimacy and subsequent enculturation. These factors, in my view, are a product of the four vulnerabilities discussed in chapter 2. In our separation from nature and the subsequent elevation of science we have developed a cultural intolerance of the not-yet-known, the unknowable, and the mysterious. Complexity and chaos is avoided, even feared. A contributing factor to this cultural intolerance has been the elevation of science, technology, and quantitative systems of knowing, combined with the devaluation of qualitative or spiritually guided systems of knowing. Science can help us develop a better appreciation of the mysterious and the unknown, but more often it becomes a tool of our fears or a deity to be worshipped. In the scientific conceptualization, all that is true or real is observable, measurable, and ultimately knowable. Anything that does not yield to these criteria is suspect. The cultural elevation of the quantitative and allegedly objective above the qualitative and subjective has contributed to the view that ambiguous social situations or problems are somehow dangerous, and possibly immoral, and should therefore be avoided.

As professionals and laypersons, we have no cultural precedent that encourages the appreciation and use of the wisdom traditions together with analytic methods. This situation leaves us inadequately prepared when approaching thorny social issues. Furthermore, a systemic analysis of a social issue is incomplete without the inclusion of the historical and cultural background that brought the community face to face with the social problem in question. An examination of a social issue in light of the four social-cultural vulnerabilities discussed in Jason's book will help reveal specifically how our aggressive tendencies, our literal and intellectual separation from nature, and our concurrent stripping of metaphor and mythology have left us vulnerable to severe social decay.

An example of an intervention model that demonstrates the eco-transformational framework is a social application of my Four-Phase Model of Social Change (for an example of a clinical application of this model to a chronically ill population, see Fennell, 1995). This four-phase process acknowledges the individual, the individual's family, workplace, social network, care provider, and general community as dynamic, interactive, and interdependent factors within an organic whole. In Phase I the social issue moves from an onset to an emergency phase, and the social task of the individual and the community is coping with trauma. In Phase II the social issue moves into the breakdown and restablization phase, and the social task of the individual and the community is the initiation of stabilization. In Phase III the social issue moves into the existential phase, and the social task is the development of meaning. In Phase IV the social issue moves into the integration phase, and the social task is integration and transcendence. At each phase a coalition of the wisdom traditions together with more behavioral approaches is utilized to help the community meet the tasks at hand and move successfully into the next phase.

Through an understanding of this paradigm, patients, families, and caregivers can experience less fear and anxiety. The unknown becomes more known as individuals locate themselves on a narrative map or experiential time line. This map serves as a tool for patients by helping them develop a sense or order of the sometimes traumatic experiences that are happening to them. As the experience of ambiguity and chaos is diminished, patients gain a degree of coherency regarding their experiences. They have a method to validate their experiences, stabilize and structure their responses, develop meaning for their experiences, and ultimately transcend them. As indicated by Jason throughout this volume, helping individuals find their path on this life journey is a critical task for people who want to build sturdy communities.

Regardless of the helping tools that are utilized in addressing a social problem, the following three transformational steps or processes are inherent in the Four-Phase Model and should be considered in the healing of personal and social issues: (1) acceptance of suffering, as opposed to its rejection and the subsequent rejection of the self; (2) development of a compassionate response to the suffering of the rejected sick, stigmatized self; and (3) development of respect for the actual act of suffering—for the time in the tunnel, not the light at the end of it. These steps create a respect for the new self. The process necessitates borrowing from the wisdom traditions and the faith of the care provider as the patient and his or her family gropes through this lengthy, frightening process. In the pit of their grief, individuals reach out to the wisdom traditions for support and find mercy for suffering, integration of pain and loss, and encouragement and grace to embrace the paradox of living. Through this experience, they may begin to consider another way to be in the world, through role and identity experimentation. This process facilitates the development of meaning for their experiences, while it creates an opportunity to begin integration of aspects of the precrisis self with the new emerging respected self. By fully embracing the shadow, as suggested by Jason in this volume, some individuals and communities may spend their financial and human resources on educational and support organizations, creative expression, political activism, or community building.

Finally, Jason's eco-transformational model integrates linear quantitative systems of evaluation and intervention with more qualitative systems of knowing and healing. My Four-Phase Model is a manifestation of this inclusive framework, which utilizes culture, context, and ecological exchange between all the actors and agents and develops meaning by employing constructs from a variety of qualitative disciplines and fields. The eco-transformational approach validates the necessity of community in the process of healing, by supporting the caregiver, and recovery, and by helping to provide the social container necessary to support the patient, families, and communities as they experience the trauma of Phase I, create stabilization in Phase II, patiently develop meaning and thus reclaim the power over their lives in Phase III, and achieve integration, connection, and community in Phase IV. As the eco-transformational approach makes clear, the health and willing involvement of one's immediate and larger communities are salient indicators of who recovers and who does not.

—Patricia A. Fennell, CSW-R
Albany Health Management Associates, Inc.

Notes

1. More recently, evolutionary psychologists have rejected notions of programmed inflexibility or environmental unmodifiability. DeKay and Buss (1992) suggest that over the centuries, when males and females confronted different adaptive problems, gender differences emerged. Jealousy in men is more likely to be aroused by threats of sexual infidelity, whereas in women jealousy appears to be aroused by the loss of a partner's commitment and investment in the relationship. The risk to the male is not knowing if he is the father of the child, whereas the female's risk is loss of the partner's resources. Gender differences in the value of relationships will be viewed from different points of view in this book; but for now, it is of interest that there may be evolutionary explanations for them.

2. Approximately five to seven million years ago, climatic changes in Africa drove chimpanzees to leave their tree homes for the grassy open plains. Creatures with the face of an ape began to walk upright, making it easier to spot enemies and prey. In 1974, Donald Johanson's discovery of the remains of Lucy, a member of a hominid species called australopithecine, provided evidence of the missing link between apes and human beings, which lived about three million years ago (Johanson & Shreeve, 1989). Lucy had an ape-like brain a little larger than that of a chimp, and she was probably a vegetarian. By walking on two feet, australopithecines could travel long distances across grasslands to new forests, and their hands were free to carry food back to their families. Just as our species has constantly adapted to changing conditions, these adaptations gave our ancestors a competitive edge on the plains of Africa.

The first primitive human beings, known as Homo habilis, whose bones were discovered by Mary Leakey in 1960, emerged about two million years ago. This was a major evolutionary leap, for this more intelligent species could make rudimentary tools. By bashing one rock against another, Homo habilis could produce a sharp stone that could be used as a cutting tool. Homo habilis may have used these stone tools to break the bones of dead animals in order to eat the nutritious marrow. Some anthropologists have claimed that this use of tools marked the dawn of human technology. These early human beings were primarily scavengers, with a largely vegetarian diet.

As more of the forests turned to grasslands in Africa, there were new competitors, including lions and packs of hunting dogs. Intelligence was the key to survival for Homo erectus, who emerged 1.5 million years ago with a skull twice the size of Lucy's. With a tall, powerful body, this ancestor of ours could travel to a carcass quickly, using the newly developed stone ax to carve up dead animals before this food was taken away by stronger hunting animals. With the discovery of fire about a million years ago, Homo erectus was able to cook food and frighten away other animals. This innovation allowed our ancestors to leave Africa and venture into colder climates.

During the Ice Age from 150,000 B.C. to 35,000 B.C., the Neanderthals roamed the earth. They used simple stone tools and buried their dead but left few hints of higher culture. The experts are divided about whether the Neanderthals were our direct ancestors or an evolutionary dead end.

3. During those primitive times, people in the colder northern areas procured food by hunting (Campbell, 1980). Archeological findings from hunter societies suggest that primitive hunters made religious pacts with the animals they hunted: If certain magical rituals and rites were performed before, during, and after the hunt, the hunters believed the animals would be reborn after dying, thus preserving an abundant supply of food (Livingston, 1989). Wilber (1995) cites evidence suggesting that, although men hunted and women were involved in food gathering and child rearing, there was no difference in status between men's and women's work. In the warm equatorial zones, where either gender could easily collect the abundant fruit and vegetables, the relative importance of the male role was reduced. In those warmer climates, female images became dominant because women brought forth life (Campbell, 1980). It was also in these climates that rites of human sacrifice became more common.

Human sacrifice is difficult for us to comprehend, yet this practice provides useful glimpses into ancient world orders (Campbell, 1980). One old custom on a Polynesian island represented the tribe's response to the passage of boys and girls into adulthood. One boy and one girl would be selected from all those reaching puberty. The youths would be killed and eaten by the villagers, who expressed joy and gratitude that their god had sacrificed itself for the tribe. When the tribe ate, they were eating the body of their god. It was with respect and reverence that they sacrificed two of their children as part of the renewal of this mystery. As horrible as this rite seems to us, it does indicate how these people resolved one of the great perplexing issues that we all confront: how to rationalize the fact that we must consume other lives in order to live, and that ultimately we are also consumed by other organisms, including predators in the wild and bacteria in decomposition. Because these people lived completely in the world of nature, they accepted this fact of nature without reservation. Even if we now find their methods abhorrent, we can understand the need for resolution.

4. In India around 2000 B.C., a civilization developed on rich land nourished by nearby rivers. In accordance with their Hindu religion, inhabitants led a strong spiritual life, believing that all life was sacred. China's great civilizations, begun around 1500 B.C., were also based on a reverence for moral and natural order and were heavily influenced by Confucius's belief in respect for the family and the law and by the Taoist principle of respect for the forces of nature best articulated by Lao Tsu. During the period from about 2500 to 500 B.C., these ideas from the Orient spoke to the goddesses of the planting people. Through the Upanishads, the teachings of Buddha, and the writings of Lao Tsu, a philosophy was given voice that emphasized being at one with the mystery of nature. These teachings did not rely on a priestly class that in other civilizations had become the intermediary for humanity's relationship with the deity; rather they spoke of a direct relationship with the almighty, and—at the highest level—of a merging with universal forces.

In the great Mayan civilization in Central America, the corn farmers originally lived in balance with nature. The Mayans were well versed in writing and astronomy; they used mathematics to predict eclipses. The Mayan cities grew and became powerful, even though they were in a state of constant warfare (Gilbert, 1995). As the population grew, houses covered the valleys and the fertile land where food had once been grown. As the land was deforested, erosion also became a significant problem. Finally, in approximately 800 A.D., plagued by severe droughts and the challenge of survival on less fertile lands, the people abandoned the great cities and began drifting back to the jungles. Because the people had disrupted their balance with nature by overworking the land, the great Mayan civilization was destroyed. Even civilizations with sophisticated cultures can fail when their people do not live in balance with the ecosystem.

5. All living beings attempt to increase their population, but nature regulates this tendency toward overpopulation by imposing checks and balances on this dynamic process. For example, if there are many predators, the number of prey decreases, resulting eventually in a reduction in the number of predators. Some might argue that it was not a reverence for nature, but the checks and balances of nature, that kept ancient civilizations from abusing the land and their resources. Even if this is true, it is still important to understand the forces that led to the development of science and technology, which provided our species with the tools to overcome the limitations imposed by nature.

6. The Aryans of the western group were the ancestors of the Greek, Latin, French, Spanish, German, English, and Celtic languages. The Aryans of the eastern group were the ancestors of the languages of Northern India, Persia, Armenia, Russia, and Poland. The Semitic groups from the Saudi Arabian desert were responsible for the languages of the Arcadians, Babylonians, Hebrews, and Arabs. The discovery and use of bronze as a weapon, and the domestication of horses, possibly gave these nomads the resources to be efficient and effective warriors.

7. The promise of a messiah destined to free the people from the grip of evil is one of the tenets of the ancient Jewish religion. The emphasis on controlling nature can also be found in the Old Testament. In a section of Genesis, God said to man:

> Be fruitful, and multiply, and replenish the earth, and subdue it; and have dominion over the fish of the sea, and over the fowl of the air, and over every living thing that creepeth upon the earth. (Gen. 1:28)

This passage clearly shows that the ancient Jews believed the world was created for our species to control and dominate.

We have argued that the impulse to control nature had many negative consequences. However, within religions that espoused this belief, there also existed many generative and powerfully constructive values and traditions. For example, the Jewish people, as absolute monotheists, took a stand against all polytheism and paganism. The notion that there was only one God, and that this was the God for all people, led to the idea that the human race was unified. This made possible the teaching of the brotherhood of all human beings, the idea of loving one's neighbor as oneself. Moral and ethical values became an integral part of Jewish religious life, and human sacrifice and other inhumanities, such as crucifixions as practiced by the Romans, were rejected. Children were regarded as the highest of human treasures, whereas in many other early cultures, children had few rights or protections (for example, the Greeks left weak children to perish exposed on mountain tops) (Hertz, 1960). In the prophetic traditions, people were instructed that they had a responsibility to the disenfranchised, the poor, and the hungry. Jews have a historical experience with oppression, and they have often felt a moral imperative to liberate the oppressed (Furman, 1991).

8. Furman (1991) provides a somewhat different interpretation of the paradise myth. Adam and Eve's actions may be paradigmatic of human freedom to choose between good and evil. In Judaism, both Adam and Eve were responsible for the act of disobedience, thus averting the frequent Christian association between Eve and the fall, and therefore between women and evil. The patriarchal roots of Judaism are universal among world religions (Furman, 1991). In Buddhism, women were subservient to men (Read, 1991), and in the Hindu system, women were burned alive after their husbands died (McCann, 1991). In the current era, many religions are undergoing major transformations in an attempt to eradicate the previous practices of discrimination toward women.

9. After the Emperor Constantine merged the Roman Empire with the Christian Church, the new religion of Catholicism spread widely. In the hierarchical universe described in that religion, God was at the highest level, followed by the angels, then by men, and finally by women, who were considered separate from and valued less than men. People's connection with the land and sense of place in their communities were still nourishing and vital, and their social and economic roles usually provided a sturdy sense of meaning. With the collapse of the Roman Empire, and the nomadic invasion of Europe, however, many of the cities were destroyed and thousands lost their lives.

During the Middle Ages, a feudalism emerged that was based on farming and loyalty to a lord or king. This hierarchy began to break down when peasants began migrating to cities. The seeds of later problems were being sown. In the 1300s the bubonic plague, or "Black Death," ravaged Europe, and up to one-third of the people in that part of the world died. From 1337 to 1453, England and France were involved in a brutal series of wars, and the Turks began to overrun Europe.

10. Putnam (1993) provides an insightful analysis of Italy, which in the me-

dieval period had the most advanced political structure in Europe. From the eleventh century onward, northern Italy relied more on horizontal collaboration than on vertical hierarchy, which was the structure typical of most monarchies at the time. Communes were formed from voluntary associations, groups of neighbors who pooled their resources for common defense and economic cooperation. Soon craftsmen and tradesmen formed guilds to provide self-help and mutual assistance. These groups pressed for political reform and greater representation on town councils. Although only a minority of the population became members of the emerging communes, they served as a starting point for popular participation in government affairs.

Gradually other local organizations were formed as well, including neighborhood associations, parish organizations, religious societies, and political parties. These groups provided a rich network of associational life. As people gained greater control in shaping their political destinies, they developed strong allegiances to their cities. New experts in municipal government emerged, and the ranks of lawyers and judges grew, in response to the need to interpret the new agreements among associations. Commerce expanded rapidly, as merchants from northern Italian cities extended their trade networks to the entire known world, from China to Greenland. A new economic revolution began, facilitated by the invention of credit, which provided an intermediary between individual savers and investors and allowed private capital to be harnessed for economic growth. Long distance trade required credit; therefore, both buyers and sellers had to have confidence in contracts and laws. Due to networks of civic engagement, which flourished in northern Italy, people were willing to invest their savings in larger commercial enterprises; this fueled the vast economic growth of cities and ultimately contributed to political and economic advances.

In sharp contrast, southern Italy—settled by Norman mercenaries—was strictly autocratic and authoritarian, never allowing the independent communes that existed in the north. As the centuries passed, the feudal monarchy persisted, with a landed aristocracy ruling poor peasant masses, bridged by a small middle class of ineffective administrators and professionals. This authoritarian political structure engendered exploitation and dependence; the states were poorly administered, and the poor peasantry was overworked and granted no civic rights.

Many of the historical events discussed below were described in Theodore K. Rabb's (1993) book *Renaissance Lives: Portraits of an Age*. In the 1300s and 1400s, city-states in Italy, such as Venice and Genoa, became powerful centers of finance. This was based on trade, much of it going through the Near East. In 1453, when the Ottoman Turks captured Constantinople, the western merchants lost many of their trading concessions to the Near East. In order to find an alternative route to the Far East, merchants in Genoa and Prince Henry of Portugal invested in voyages of exploration down the west coast of Africa. Columbus's explorations across the Atlantic, supported by Queen Isabella of Spain, were also efforts to find an alternative trade route to China.

The powerful city-states of Venice and Genoa began inventing techniques of modern industry. With patronage from the traders, architecture and art flourished. The Renaissance artists looked at the world with new eyes and greater precision and sparked a rebirth of interest in the ancient Greek and Roman civilizations. In 1453 Gutenberg invented the printing press. As a result, more people learned to read and to explore the world of ideas that was previously reserved for a few privileged scholars. In Florence, Machiavelli wrote about how a ruler could manipulate perceptions in order to gain power. The Italian cities were dominated by powerful families, each ruthless clan struggling to crush the others. A new class of capitalists was emerging, with money as their primary value and their source of power.

Spain, Portugal, and the Italian city-states profited from new trade routes to the New World, selling slaves from Africa for the gold, silver, and other resources plundered in the Americas. The destructive capacity of gunpowder, a substance originally invented by the Chinese, gave the European soldiers a clear advantage over African and New World populations. Spears and arrows were no match against muskets and cannons. At the expense of the populations of other continents, this trade led to an enormous expansion in wealth and resources for Spain and other European trading countries.

King Philip II of Spain developed new ways of maintaining order and control over his rivals and his people. His subjects were told that their existence could be maintained only through service to their country. New laws were passed, and a bureaucracy was established to collect taxes from the local citizens. The power of the prince and the central state were now used to keep a large realm united.

After the British defeat of the Spanish navy in 1588, Northeastern European countries became the preeminent powers. The produce of the world was now being transported to Amsterdam and London. New agricultural techniques, such as crop rotation and better methods of livestock management, were developed, and plants from the New World, such as the potato, were introduced. These developments led to a greater and more stable food supply, allowing the Northeastern European population to expand.

11. In the 1300s the Church was the authority, and from birth to death there were rules for life that would guarantee access to salvation. However, some Catholics began to notice that a variety of practices within the Roman Catholic Church differed from those taught by Jesus Christ as reported in the New Testament. For example, in 1403 Jan Huss asserted that Christ had preached that everyone, not just the priests (as was the practice in the Roman Church), could drink wine from the chalice. After criticizing the purchase of indulgences for gold and silver as a substitute for true repentance, Huss was burned at the stake. Martin Luther read the sermons of Huss, and by 1517 he was preaching that the scriptures did not set forth the requirement that an intermediary translate between God and man. The believer needed only faith and a Bible; the Church was not required (Brecht, 1990). Dissent began spreading to all segments of the population, and serfs began to realize that they were born free in the sight of God. In revolts all over Germany, more than 120,000 peasants were killed. Even though at this point Luther had become reactionary, siding with the princes, this new appreciation for dissent had become one of the most liberating elements of the Renaissance. Freedom of expression fueled a growing rejection of political tyranny and opened the world of ideas for exploration.

In the 1400s, natural philosophers were studying and debating the works of the past. Their speculations were intimately tied to the teachings of the Christian Church. Their passion to understand God's expression through nature helped them create new ways of seeing and understanding nature; this led to the emergence of science. Copernicus was the first to propound the theory that the sun, rather than the earth, was the center of the universe; however, his audience was very limited, and he lacked the evidence to prove his theory. In the 1600s Kepler found evidence that the planets' orbits were elliptical, and that the sun was at their center. In 1610 Galileo published his discoveries, which were possible because of the telescope, a new instrument that joined technology with theory. Galileo collected persuasive evidence that the earth did in fact revolve around the sun. Yielding to Church pressure, he recanted his theory in 1633.

12. It was not long before intellectual prowess and achievement became the primary symbols of success. The Protestant work ethic emphasized achievement as evidence of righteousness, and efforts to achieve were often directed at controlling nature and opposing the forces of evil. In addition, as pointed out by Bartel and Guskin (1971), notions of equality from the French Revolution were paired with an obligation to take advantage of the opportunity to be equal. If one did not succeed, one's social stakes and reputation tended to suffer.

13. Even though religious beliefs have been challenged by scientific discoveries, many people have continued to maintain allegiance to some religious organization, although formal participation in religious services may be perfunctory. Ladd (1993/94) claims that in the United States there is a persistent strength of religious belief, and a 1981 Gallup poll indicated that 79 percent of Americans gained strength from religion. Hayes and Lipset (1993/94) also maintain that the majority of Americans continue to take an active role in their local religious communities. It is important, however, to distinguish a willingness to engage in occasional religious festivities and rituals from a deeper intrinsic commitment and faith; this difference will be explored further in later chapters.

14. Both the contextual model and the post-modern deconstructive model posit that an understanding of any phenomenon is based on cultural relativity. In other words, neither model asserts the existence of foundational values. Ecological post-modernists, on the other hand, believe that there are hundreds of varieties of foundational values and that these values increase meaning, vitality, energy, connection, and authenticity. A key question is whether one can have foundational values and be culturally relativistic but not espouse deconstructive post-modernism. It may be possible to be culturally relativistic and foundational as long as these different viewpoints on reality have their sources within foundational values. Immanual Kant believed that the choice of moral values was not solvable by scientific thought because only objects of experience could be known. However, in his *Critique of Practical Reason* (1788), he maintained that morality required a belief in the existence of these values. If we assume that moral values pertain to particular cultural groups (cultural relativism), then we should extend these values and apply them to other groups. Thus foundational values would become relevant to humanity.

15. There has been a tendency among psychologists to develop instruments that tap negative psychological traits, although there are some psychologists who have focused more on health-promoting psychological attitudes such as life purpose and satisfaction (Kass et al., 1991). Antonovsky (1987) suggests that we need a salutogenic orientation, one that focuses on how people move to the positive end of the health–disease continuum. To this end, he has developed the sense of coherence concept, which describes an enduring feeling of confidence that one's

environment is predictable and that things will work out as well as can be reasonably expected.

16. Scientists from the MacArthur Foundation Research Network on Successful Midlife Development, including Ronald Kessler, Margie Lachman, Gilbert Brim, David Featherman, and Paul Baltes, suggest that middle age can be the best time in one's life. In summarizing their work, Gallagher (1993) writes that during these years, most individuals are healthy and productive, have enough money to do the things they like, and don't have to deal with the anxieties of youth or the pains of old age. Even though many in middle age have a lot going on, they are at their peak in terms of competence and ability to handle stress. The majority of people come to terms with their finite resources in a gentle rather than a painful process, by adopting practical goals (using their brains and skills rather than physical prowess) or substituting alternate goals (if work is not satisfying, some people focus on satisfactions from other facets of life, such as home and family). Only 10 to 12 percent of respondents report having a midlife crisis, and most of these individuals experienced internal upheavals throughout their lives. By midlife, the majority of respondents report being more or less content. Most people seem to maintain a manageable life through the years. They do this by constantly resetting goals that demand about 80 percent of their capacity; pushing beyond that level leads to stress, anxiety, and burnout.

In this book, I argue that there has been a significant breakdown in the psychological sense of community in contemporary society. Yet the findings of eminent researchers on midlife adjustment suggest that this has not occurred. There are several ways of interpreting this difference. It is possible that the breakdown in a sense of community has occurred only for a minority (10 to 12 percent) of the population, and that the majority is relatively content. It is also possible that the samples used by Kessler et al. were biased toward an affluent, middle-class population, and that many more individuals—particularly those with fewer resources—are experiencing this breakdown in the sense of community. Finally, the quantitative methods used to gather much of the midlife data may have missed the qualitative picture of the deeper and more troubling issues confronting our citizens. For example, a man may express high levels of personal satisfaction by channeling all of his time and energy into his work; yet at a deeper level, his life may be imbalanced, his family may feel neglected, and his contribution to the significant issues facing his neighborhood may be minimal.

17. They used five criteria to characterize wisdom-related knowledge: factual knowledge about fundamental life matters, procedural knowledge about dealing with life problems, life span contextualism, relativism of values and life goals, and recognition and management of uncertainty. To tap these domains, people were asked to think aloud about vignettes describing life problems, and their responses were tape recorded and later rated on the five criteria. Most individuals performed only in the average range on the wisdom-related criteria.

18. Hood (1977) has been among the most prolific students of mysticism and intense religious experiences. In developing the Religious Experience Episodes Measure (REEM), he culled reports of religious experiences from the writings of William James and then edited 15 experiences (Hood, 1970). To measure the degree of reported religious experience, each of these experiences was rated on a five-point scale. Individuals who measured high on psychological strength

were more likely to report intense religious experiences (Hood, 1974). Hood (1975) also developed a Mysticism Scale to measure reported mystical experiences. Two factors emerged from the 32–item scale. Factor 1 was an indicator of an intense experience, such as unity, inner subjectivity or ineffability, and factor 2 measured the joyful expression of traditionally defined religious experiences. The Mysticism Scale had a significant positive correlation with the REEM, and a measure of openness to experience. Persons reporting mystical experiences can be described as creative and innovative, tolerant of others, socially adept, and unwilling to accept simplistic or incomplete solutions to problems (Hood, Hall, Watson, Biderman, 1979).

Several other scales have been developed to measure spirituality. For example, Ellison (1983) has developed a Spiritual Well-Being Scale that has two dimensions: sense of well-being in relation to God, and sense of life purpose and satisfaction. Kass, Friedman, Leserman, Zuttermeister, and Benson (1991) have developed the Index of Core Spiritual Experience. Items on the scale include the conviction that God exists, and the attitudes that are present when people believe that God either is close to them or is dwelling within them. This instrument is related to increased life purpose and decreased frequency of medical symptoms.

19. Not all agree that we are presently confronted with a breakdown in the sense of community. For example, Lyon (1989) suggests that there is little evidence to support the claim of individual alienation and further claims that much Gemeinschaft remains in contemporary society. Lyon further states that efforts that rely on conflict to revitalize neighborhoods through community development, such as the work of Alinsky (1969), have had limited success because they are difficult to implement and because they require the time-consuming and continuous efforts of a community organizer. Lyon recommends two other approaches: self-help and technical assistance. In the self-help approach, a facilitator brings people together, and the people then decide what needs to be done. In the technical assistance approach, an outside expert provides skills to help guide and evaluate the community development process. Lyon considers both approaches to be useful strategies for building a stronger sense of community. He also suggests that Gemeinschaft qualities can be enhanced through efforts to strengthen voluntary organizations, and that these organizations can provide a needed sense of belonging.

Some also suggest that in response to America's social decay, a renewed interest in community is in evidence (*Economist*, 1995). Decreasing crime rates are sometimes cited as proof of this trend. However, decreasing crime might be the result of improvement in the economy; decreasing numbers of teenagers, the age group most likely to commit crimes; and longer prison terms for criminals. The fact that the prison guard's position is one of the fastest growing occupations in this country is, however, an ominous sign (over 1.5 million Americans are currently behind bars).

20. McMillan and Chavis (1986) defined this concept as having four elements: a feeling of belonging, a sense of making a difference, shared emotional connections, and a feeling that members' needs will be met. Dunham (1986) suggested that this concept should not be limited to the notion of place, but rather that it was better conceived as a process than a fixed geographic location.

Glynn (1981) was the first to develop a scale to measure the psychological sense of community, which he considered a common bond with other people. Glynn found that the number of years one expected to live in a community, and the number of neighbors one could identify by first name, were strong contributors to a perceived sense of community. His scale taps both the actual and the ideal senses of community and is tied to a certain place. Doolittle and MacDonald (1978), Chavis, Hogge, McMillan, and Wandersman (1986), and Buckner (1988) also developed scales to measure sense of community, and their scales were also tied to a particular place.

One of the problems with scales that measure sense of community is that many of their items tap concepts that could be thought of as either the causal roots or outcomes of sense of community (Chertok, personal communication, 7 April 1992). Chertok further notes that most of the scales mix items that tap different levels of analysis. They also include items such as commonly held beliefs and attributes of the setting.

21. In brief, Kelly has proposed four ecological principles that can serve as a conceptual framework for examining settings and behavior: interdependence, cycling of resources, adaptation, and succession. Interdependence indicates that any change in one component of an ecosystem can effect changes in relationships among other components of the system as well. The principle of cycling of resources provides a guide for understanding how ecosystems create and use new resources. It allows us to determine how resources can be used more effectively in a setting and how additional resources can be generated. Adaptation is the principle that environments shape people's methods of adaptation. A behavior that is adaptive in one setting may not be adaptive in others. This principle points us toward trying to assess who participates in defining the adaptive roles and toward generating normative acceptance and support for a wide range of adaptive behaviors. Finally, the principle of succession suggests that communities are in a constant process of change, and that over time the demand for adaptive capacities changes. While these principles focus on different aspects of the social context and behavior, they also overlap and complement each other.

References

Abdul-Adil, J. K., & Jason, L. A. (1991). Community Psychology and Al-Islam: A religious framework for social change. *The Community Psychologist, 24,* 28–30.

Adams, R. E. (1992). Is happiness a home in the suburbs? The influence of urban versus suburban neighborhoods on psychological health. *Journal of Community Psychology, 20,* 353–371.

Adelman, M. B., & Frey, L. R. (1994). The pilgrim must embark: Creating and sustaining community in a residential facility for people with AIDS. In L. R. Frey (Ed.), *Group communication in context: Studies of natural groups* (pp. 3–22). Hillsdale, NJ: Lawrence Erlbaum.

Adelman, M. B., & Frey, L. R. (1997). *The fragile community: Living together with AIDS*. Mahwah, NJ: Lawrence Erlbaum.

Ader, R., & Cohen, N. (1975). Behaviorally conditioned immunosuppression. *Psychosomatic Medicine, 37,* 333–340.

Adler, A. (1951). *The practice and theory of individual psychology*. Totowa, NJ: Littlefield, Adams.

Albee, G. W. (1986). Toward a just society. *American Psychologist, 41,* (8), 891–898.

Albee, G. W. (1996). Revolutions and counterrevolutions in prevention. *American Psychologist, 51,* 1130–1133.

Alinsky, S. (1969). *Reveille for radicals*. New York: Vintage.

Allport, G. W. & Ross, J. M. (1967). Personal religious orientation and prejudice. *Journal of Personality and Social Psychology, 5,* (4), 432–443.

American Association for Protecting Children (1987, October 23). *National estimates of child abuse and neglect reports, 1976–1986*. Denver: American Humane Association.

Anderson, S., & Hopkins, P. (1992). *The feminine face of God*. New York: Bantam.

Antonovsky, A. (1987). *Unraveling the mystery of health: How people manage stress and stay well.* San Francisco: Jossey-Bass.

Arrien, A. (1993). *The four-fold way: Walking the paths of the warrior, teacher, healer, and visionary.* San Francisco: Harper.

Assagioli, R. (1965). *Psychosynthesis.* New York: Viking Compass.

Barker, R. G. (1968). *Ecological Psychology.* Stanford, CA: Stanford University.

Barnes, H. (1985). The heroic paradox. *Contemporary Literature, 37,* 269–276.

Bartel, N. R., & Guskin, S. L. (1971). A handicap as a social phenomenon. In W. M. Cruickshank (Ed.), *Psychology of exceptional children* (pp. 75–114). Englewood Cliffs, NJ: Prentice-Hall.

Batson, C. D., & Ventis, W. L. (1982). *The religious experience. A social-psychological perspective.* New York: Oxford University Press.

Baumeister, R. F., & Leary, M. R. (1995). The need to belong: Desire for interpersonal attachments as a fundamental human motivation. *Psychological Bulletin, 117,* 497–529.

Bellah, R. N., Madsen, R., Sullivan, W. M., Swidler, A., & Tipton, S. M. (1985). *Habits of the heart: Individualism and commitment in American life.* New York: Harper & Row.

Bellah, R. N., Madsen, R., Sullivan, W. M., Swidler, A., & Tipton, S. M. (1991). *The good society.* New York: Knopf.

Benson, H., & Stuart, E. N. (1992). *The wellness book: The comprehensive guide to maintaining health and treating stress-related illness.* New York: Birch Lane.

Berry, T. (1988). *The dream of the earth.* San Francisco: Sierra Club Books.

Biglan, A. (1995). *Changing cultural practice: A contextualist framework for intervention research.* Reno, NV: Context Press.

Bishop, P., Chertok, F., & Jason, L. A. (in press). Factor analysis of a scale measuring the psychological sense of community. *Journal of Primary Prevention.*

Blank, W. (1993). Torah & tantra: Parallel paths to the experience of god. *Ecstasy Journal, 2* (2), 27–32.

Blumenkrantz, D. G., & Gavazze, S. M. (1993). Guiding transitional events for children and adolescents through a modern day rite of passage. *The Journal of Primary Prevention, 13,* 199–212.

Borysenko, J. (1993). *The powers of the mind to heal.* Cassette Recording. Niles, IL: Nightingale Conant Corporation.

Bower, B. (1991). Questions of mind over immunity. *Science News, 139,* 216–217.

Bradshaw, J. (1990). *Homecoming: Reclaiming and championing your inner child.* New York: Bantam Books.

Brecht, M. (1990). *Martin Luther, shaping and defining the Reformation 1521–1532.* Minneapolis: Fortress Press.

Briggs, B. B. (1993). Transforming ritual. *Conscious Choice, 6,* 36–37.

Briggs, J., & Peat, F. D. (1989). *Turbulent mirror: An illustrated guide to chaos theory and the science of wholeness.* New York: Harper & Row.

Brooke, T. (1986). *Riders of the cosmic circuit.* Batavia, IL: Lion Publications.

Bry, B. H., Hirsch, B. J., Newbrough, J. R., Reischl, T. M., & Swindle, R. W. (1990). Criteria of excellence II. Hypothesis generation: Human science and attribute-centered social regularities. In P. Tolan, C. Keys, F. Chertok, & L. Jason (Eds.), *Researching community psychology: Issues of theory and methods* (pp. 101–108). Washington, DC: American Psychological Association.

Buckner, J. C. (1988). The development of an instrument to measure neighborhood cohesion. *American Journal of Community Psychology, 16*, 771–791.

Burkhardt, M. A. (1989). Spirituality: An analysis of the concept. *Holistic Nursing Practice, 3* (3), 69–77.

Campbell, J. (1949). *The hero with a thousand faces*. New York: Pantheon.

Campbell, J. (1969). The world mythology series. Cassette Recording. Big Sur, CA: Dolphin Tapes.

Campbell, J. (1971). Hermes, alchemy, and the voyage of Odysseus. Cassette Recording. Big Sur, CA: Dolphin Tapes.

Campbell, J. (1980). Transformation of myth through time. Volume II. Cassette Recording. Big Sur, CA: Dolphin Tapes.

Campbell, J. (1990). *The flight of the wild gander*. New York: Harper Perennial.

Camus, A. (1982). *The stranger*. (Kate Griffith, Trans.). Washington, DC: University Press of America.

Cannon, W. (1935). Stresses and strains of homeostasis. *American Journal of the Medical Sciences, 189*, 1–14.

Caplan, G. (1964). *Principles of preventive psychiatry*. New York: Basic Books.

Castaneda, C. (1973). *The teachings of Don Juan*. New York: Simon & Schuster.

Cavalieri, P., & Singer, P. (1994). *The great ape project: Equality beyond humanity*. New York: St. Martin's Press.

Chamberlin, J. (1996). Self-help: Living it, promoting it, and learning from it. *The Community Psychologist, 29*, 10–11.

Chaudhuri, H. (1991). In C. T. Hart (Ed.), *Transpersonal psychologies: Perspectives on the mind from seven great spiritual traditions* (pp. 231–280). New York: HarperCollins.

Chavis, D. M., Hogge, J. H., McMillan, D. W., & Wandersman, A. (1986). Sense of community through Brunswick's lens: A first look. *Journal of Community Psychology, 14*, 24–40.

Chodorow, N. (1974). Family structure and feminine personality. In M. Z. Rosaldo & L. Lamphere (Eds.), *Women, culture and society*. Stanford, CA: Stanford University Press.

Chopra, D. (1990). *Quantum healing: Exploring the frontiers of mind/body medicine*. New York: Bantam Books.

Chopra, D. (1994). *The seven spiritual laws of success: A practical guide to the fulfillment of your dreams*. San Rafael, CA: New World Library.

Cohen, S., & Williamson, G. M. (1991). Stress and disease in humans. *Psychological Bulletin, 109*, 5–24.

Cook, T. D., & Shadish, W. R. (1986). Program evaluation. The worldly science. In M. R. Rosenzweig & L. W. Porter (Eds.), *Annual review of psychology* (pp. 193–232). Palo Alto, CA: Annual Reviews, Inc.

Copernicus, N. (1995). *On the revolutions of heavenly spheres* (C. G. Wallis, Trans.). New York: Prometheus Books. (Original work published 1543.)

Cornford, F. M. (1966). *The republic of Plato*. New York: Oxford University Press.

Cottrell, L. (1976). The competent community. In B. H. Kaplan, R. N. Wilson & A. H. Leighton (Eds.), *Further explorations in social psychiatry* (pp. 195–209). New York: Basic Books.

Cousins, N. (1989). *Head first: The biology of hope*. New York: E. P. Dutton.

Cowan, J. (1993). *The common table: Reflections and meditations on community and spirituality in the workplace.* New York: Harper Business.

Crawford, I., Jason, L. A., Riordan, N., Kaufman, J., Salina, D., Sawalski, L., Ho, F. C., & Zolik, E. (1990). A multi-media based approach to increasing communication and the level of AIDS knowledge within families. *Journal of Community Psychology, 18,* 361–373.

Csikszentmihalyi, M. (1990). *Flow: The psychology of optimal experience.* New York: HarperCollins.

Da Free, J. (1984). *The transmission of doubt.* Clearlake, CA: The Dawn Horse Press.

Darwin, C. A. (1936). *The origin of species.* New York: Modern Library. (Original work published 1859.)

Davidson, W. B., & Cotter, P. R. (1989). Sense of community and political participation. *Journal of Community Psychology, 17,* 119–125.

DeKay, W. T., & Buss, D. M. (1992). Human nature, individual differences, and the importance of context: Perspectives from evolutionary psychology. *Current Directions in Psychological Science, 1* (6), 184–189.

Diener, E., & Diener, C. (1996). Most people are happy. *Psychological Science, 7,* 181–185.

Dobyne, L., & Crawford-Mason, C. (1991). *Quality or else.* Boston: Houghton Mifflin.

Doniger, W. (1992, February 2). A very strange enchanted boy [Review of J. Campbell's *A fire in the mind*]. *New York Times Book Review,* 7–8.

Doolittle, R. J., & MacDonald, D. (1978). Communication and a sense of community in a metropolitan neighborhood: A factor analytic examination. *Communication Quarterly, 26* (3), 2–7.

Dreher, H. (1995). *The immune power personality.* New York: Dutton.

Duffy, K. G., & Wong, F. Y. (1996). *Community psychology.* Boston: Allyn and Bacon.

Dugger, R. (1995, 14/21 August). A call to citizens: Real populists please stand up. *The Nation, 261* (5), 159–164.

Dunham, H. W. (1986). The community today: Place or process. *Journal of Community Psychology, 14,* 399–404.

Dunne, J. (1986). Sense of community in l'Arche and in the writings of Jean Vanier. *Journal of Community Psychology, 14,* 41–54.

Dvorchak, P. A., Grams, G., Tate, L., & Jason, L. A. (1995). Pregnant and postpartum women in recovery: Barriers to treatment and the role of Oxford House in the continuation of care. *Alcoholism Treatment Quarterly, 13,* 97–107.

Economist, The (1995, 18 February). The solitary bowler (volunteerism and association membership in U.S.). Vol. 334, pp. 21–22.

Ellison, C. W. (1983). Spiritual well-being: Conceptualization and measurement. *Journal of Psychology and Theology, 11* (4), 330–340.

Epstein, I. (1959). *Judaism: A historical presentation.* Baltimore, MD: Penguin Books.

Erikson, E. H. (1959). Identity and the life cycle: Selected papers. *Psychological Issues, 1,* 50–100.

Etzioni, A. (1993). *The spirit of community.* New York: Crown.

Fairweather, G. W. (1979). Experimental development and dissemination of an alternative to psychiatric hospitalization: Scientific methods for social change. In R. F. Munzo, L. R. Snowden, & J. G. Kelly (Eds.), *Social and psychological research in community settings* (pp. 305–342). San Francisco: Jossey-Bass.

Fawcett, S. B. (1990). Some emerging standards for community research and action: Aid from a behavioral perspective. In P. Tolan, C. Keys, F. Chertok, & L. A. Jason (Eds.), *Researching community psychology: Issues of theory and methods* (pp. 64–75). Washington, DC: American Psychological Association.

Fawcett, S. B., Seekins, T., & Jason, L. A. (1987). Policy research and child passenger safety legislation: A case study and experimental evaluation. *Journal of Social Issues, 43,* 133–148.

Fennell, P. A. (1995). CFS, sociocultural influences and trauma: Clinical considerations. *Journal of Chronic Fatigue Syndrome, 1,* 159–173.

Fennell, P. A. (1995). The four progressive stages of the CFS experience: A coping tool for patients. *Journal of Chronic Fatigue Syndrome, 1,* 69–79.

Ferrari, J. R., Billows, W., & Jason, L. A. (1997). Matching the needs of the homeless with those of the disabled: Empowerment through caregiving. *Journal of Prevention and Intervention in the Community, 15,* 83–92.

Fowler, J. W. (1982). *Stages of faith: The psychology of human development and the quest for meaning.* San Francisco: Harper & Row.

Fox, D. R. (1993). Psychological jurisprudence and radical social change. *American Psychologist, 48* (3), 234–241.

Frankl, V. E. (1983). Meaninglessness: A challenge to psychologists. In T. Millon (Ed.), *Theories of personality and psychopathology* (3rd ed.) (pp. 256–263). New York: Holt, Rinehart & Winston.

Freud, S. (1901). *The psychopathology of everyday life.* New York: Norton, 1960.

Friedman, M. (1986). Foreword. In R. C. Arnett, *Communication and community: Implications of Martin Buber's dialogue* (pp. vii–xix). Carbondale: Southern Illinois University Press.

Fuller, R. B. (1975). *Synergetics: Explorations in the geometry of thinking.* New York: Macmillan.

Furman, F. K. (1991). Judaism. In J. D. Crossan (Ed.), *Religious worlds: Primary readings in comparative perspective* (pp. 283–349). Dubuque, IA: Kendall/Hunt Pub.

Gaines, S. O., & Reed, E. S. (1995). Prejudice: From Allport to DuBois. *American Psychologist, 50,* 96–103.

Gallagher, W. (1993, May). Midlife myths. *The Atlantic Monthly, 271* (5), 51–68.

Gelernter, C. Q. (1994, 17 April). Oxford house. *The Seattle Times,* p. M1.

Gerber, R. (1988). *Vibrational medicine.* Santa Fe, NM: Bear & Company.

Gergen, K. J. (1991). *The saturated self: Dilemmas of identity in contemporary life.* New York: Basic Books.

Gesten, E. L., & Jason, L. A. (1987). Social and community interventions. *Annual Review of Psychology, 38,* 427–460.

Gilbert, A. (1995). *The Mayan prophecies: Unlocking the secrets of a lost civilization.* Rockport, MA: Element.

Gilligan, C. (1982). *In a different voice: Psychological theory and women's development.* Cambridge, MA: Harvard University Press.

Glynn, T. J. (1981). Psychological sense of community: Measurement and application. *Human Relations, 34* (7), 789–818.

Goldman, D. (1995). *Emotional intelligence.* New York: Bantam.

Goleman, D. (1992). The Buddha on meditation and states of consciousness. In C. T. Tart (Ed.), *Transpersonal Psychologies* (pp. 203–230). New York: HarperCollins.

Goleman, D., & Gurin, J. (Eds.)? (1993). *Mind body medicine: How to use your mind for better health.* Yonkers, NY: Consumer Reports.

Goyeche, J.R.M. (1977). Yoga as therapy in psychosomatic medicine. *Psychotherapy and Psychosomatics, 31,* 373–381.

Graves, R. (1966). *The white goddess.* New York: Farrar, Straus & Giroux.

Greeley, A. M. (1974). *Ecstasy: A way of knowing.* Englewood Cliffs, NJ: Prentice-Hall.

Hanna, F. J., and Ottens, A. J. (1995). The role of wisdom in psychotherapy. *Journal of Psychotherapy Integration, 5,* 195–219.

Hay, D., & Morisy, A. (1978). Reports of ecstatic, paranormal, or religious experience in Great Britain and the United States—A comparison of trends. *Journal for the Scientific Study of Religion, 17,* (3), 255–268.

Hay, L. L. (1993). *What I believe/Deep relaxation.* Santa Monica, CA: Hay House.

Hayes, J. W., & Lipset, S. M. (1993/94). Individualism: A double-edged sword. *The Responsive Community, 4* (1), 69–80.

Heinze, R. I. (1990). *Shamans of the twentieth century.* New York: Irvington.

Heney, C., Banks, C., & Zimbardo, P. (1973). Interpersonal dynamics in a simulated prison. *International Journal of Criminology and Penology, 1,* 69–97.

Hertz, J. H. (Ed.). (1960). *The Pentateuch and Haftorahs* (2nd ed.). London: Soncino Press.

Hobfoll, S. (1988). *The ecology of stress.* New York: Hemisphere.

Hoff, Benjamin. (1982). *The Tao of Pooh.* New York: Dunton.

Hood, R. W., Jr. (1970). Religious orientation and the report of religious experience. *Journal for the Scientific Study of Religion, 9* (4), 285–291.

Hood, R. W., Jr. (1974). Psychological strength and the report of intense religious experience. *Journal for the Scientific Study of Religion, 13* (1), 65–71.

Hood, R. W., Jr. (1975). The construction and preliminary validation of a measure of reported mystical experience. *Journal for the Scientific Study of Religion, 14* (1), 29–41.

Hood, R. W., Jr. (1977). Differential triggering of mystical experience as a function of self actualization. *Review of Religious Research, 18* (3), 264–270.

Hood, R. W., Jr., Hall, J. R., Watson, P. J., & Biderman, M. (1979). Personality correlates of the report of mystical experience. *Psychological Reports, 44* (1), 804–806.

Hope, A., & Timmel, S. (1985). *Training for transformation. A handbook for community workers.* Gweru, Zimbabwe: Mambo Press.

Horney, K. (1970). *Neurosis and human growth: The struggle toward self-realization.* New York: Norton.

Housing Opportunities & Maintenance for the Elderly. (1991). Brochure. Chicago, IL.

Houston, J. (1992). *The hero and the goddess: The Odyssey as mystery and initiation.* New York: Ballantine Books.

Huxley, A. (1946). *Brave New World*. New York: Harper & Row.

Intentional Communities: A guide to cooperative living. (1990). Evansville, IN: Fellowship for Intentional Community.

Jason, L. A. (1979). Preventive community interventions: Reducing school children's smoking and decreasing smoke exposure. *Professional Psychology, 10*, 744–752.

Jason, L. A. (1984). Developing undergraduates' skills in behavioral interventions. *Journal of Community Psychology, 12*, 130–139.

Jason, L. A. (1985). Using a token-activated timer to reduce television viewing. *Journal of Applied Behavior Analysis, 18*, 269–272.

Jason, L. A. (1993). Chronic Fatigue Syndrome: New hope from psychoneuroimmunology and community psychology. *Journal of Primary Prevention, 14*, 51–71.

Jason, L. A., Berk, M., Schnopp-Wyatt, D. L., & Talbot, B. (1997). *Effects of enforcement of youth access laws on smoking prevalence*. Manuscript submitted for publication.

Jason, L. A., Curran, T., Goodman, D., & Smith, M. (1989). A media-based stress management intervention. *Journal of Community Psychology, 17*, 155–165.

Jason, L. A., Ferrari, J. R., Smith, B., Marsh, P., Dvorchak, P. A., Groessl, E. J., Pechota, M. E., Curtin, M., Bishop, P. D., Kot, E., & Bowden, B. S. (in press). An exploratory study of male recovering substance abusers living in a self-help, self-governed setting. *Journal of Mental Health Administration*.

Jason, L. A., Greiner, B., Naylor, K., Johnson, S., & Van Egeren, L. (1991). A large-scale, short-term, media-based weight loss program. *American Journal of Health Promotion, 5*, 432–437.

Jason, L. A., Gruder, C. L., Buckenberger, L., Lesowitz, T., Belgradan, J., Flay, B. R., & Warnecke, R. B. (1987). A 12-month follow-up of a worksite smoking cessation intervention. *Health Education Research, 2*, 185–194.

Jason, L. A., Gruder, C. L., Martino, S., Flay, B. R., Warnecke, R., & Thomas, N. (1987). Worksite group meetings and the effectiveness of a televised smoking cessation intervention. *American Journal of Community Psychology, 15*, 57–72.

Jason, L. A., & Hanaway, E. K. (1997). *Remote control: A sensible approach to kids, TV, and the new electronic media*. Sarasota, FL: Professional Resource Press.

Jason, L. A., Ji, P. Y., Anes, M. D., & Birkhead, S. H. (1991). Active enforcement of cigarette control laws in the prevention of cigarette sales to minors. *Journal of the American Medical Association, 266*, 3159–3161.

Jason, L. A., Ji, P. Y., Anes, M. D., & Xaverious, P. (1992). Assessing cigarette sales rates to minors. *Evaluation and the Health Professions, 15*, (4), 375–384.

Jason, L. A., & Klich, M. (1982). Intervening to alter inappropriate advertising in the mass media. *Behavioral Community Psychology, 1*, 9–16.

Jason, L. A., & Kobayashi, R. B. (1995). Community building: Our next frontier. *Journal of Primary Prevention, 15*, 195–208.

Jason, L. A., & Lattimore, B. (1990). Strengthening a religious social support system: A brief report. *Journal of Psychology and Theology, 18*, 83–85.

Jason, L. A., Lesowitz, T., Michaels, M., Blitz, C., Victors, L., Dean, L., & Yeager, E. (1989). A worksite smoking cessation intervention involving the media and incentives. *American Journal of Community Psychology, 17*, 785–799.

Jason, L. A., McMahon, S. D., Salina, D., Hedeker, D., Stockton, M., Dunson, K., & Kimball, P. (1995). Assessing a smoking cessation intervention involving groups, incentives, and self-help manuals. *Behavior Therapy, 26,* 393–408.

Jason, L. A., Pechota, M. E., Bowden, B., Kohner, K., Pokorny, S. B., Bishop, P., Quintana, E., Sangerman, C., Salina, D., Taylor, S., Lesondak, L., & Grams, G. (1994). Oxford House: Community living is community healing. In J. A. Lewis (Ed.), *Addictions: Concepts and strategies for treatment* (pp. 333–338). Gaithersburg, MD: Aspen.

Jason, L. A., Pokorny, S. B., Lahmar, K., & Bennetto, L. (1994). An evaluation of the short-term impact of a media-based substance abuse prevention program. *Journal of Community & Applied Social Psychology, 4,* 63–69.

Jason, L. A., Reichler, A., King, C., Madsen, D., Camacho, J., & Marchese, W. (1997). *The reliability and validity of the foundational value scale.* Manuscript submitted for publication.

Jason, L. A., & Rose, T. (1984). Influencing the passage of child passenger restraint legislation. *American Journal of Community Psychology, 12,* 485–495.

Jason, L. A., Salina, D., Hedeker, D., Kimball, P., Kaufman, J., Bennett, P., Bernstein, R., & Lesondak, L. (1991). Designing an effective worksite smoking cessation program using self-help manuals, incentives, groups and media. *Journal of Business Psychology, 6,* 155–166.

Jason, L. A., & Savio, D. (1978). Reducing cigarette smoke in an office setting. *Health Values, 2,* 180–185.

Jason, L. A., Tait, E., Goodman, D., Buckenberger, L., & Gruder, C. L. (1988). Effects of a televised smoking cessation intervention among low-income and minority smokers. *American Journal of Community Psychology, 16,* 863–876.

Jason, L. A., Weine, A. W., Johnson, J. H., Warren-Sohlberg, L., Filippelli, L. A., Turner, E. Y., & Lardon, C. (1992). *Helping transfer students.* San Francisco: Jossey-Bass.

Jason, L. A., & Zolik, E. S. (1985). Stimulus control and modelling strategies for controlling urban dog litter. *Urban Ecology, 9,* 63–73.

Jason, L. A., Zolik, E. S., & Matese, F. J. (1979). Prompting dog owners to pick up dog droppings. *American Journal of Community Psychology, 7,* 339–351.

Johanson, D., & Shreeve, J. (1989). *Lucy's child: The discovery of a human ancestor.* New York: Morrow.

Johanson, G., & Kurtz, R. (1991). *Grace unfolding: Psychotherapy in the spirit of the Tao-te-Ching.* New York: Bell Tower.

Joyce, J. (1993). *A portrait of the artist as a young man/James Joyce.* (H. W. Gabler & W. Hettche, Eds.). New York: Garland.

Jung, C. G. (1956). *Collected works: Vol. 5. Symbols of transformation.* Princeton, NJ: Princeton University Press.

Kabat-Zinn, J. (1991). *Full catastrophe living: Using the wisdom of your body and mind to face stress, pain, and illness.* New York: Delacorte.

Kant, I. (1788). *Critique of practical reason, and other writings in moral philosophy.* Translated and edited by Lewis White Beck. New York: Garland, 1976.

Kanter, R. M. (1972). *Commitment and community, communes and utopias in sociological perspective.* Cambridge, MA: Harvard University Press.

Kasl, S. V., Evans, A. S., & Niederman, J. C. (1979). Psychosocial risk factors in the development of infectious mononucleosis. *Psychosomatic Medicine, 41* (6), 445–466.

Kass, J. D., Friedman, R., Leserman, J., Caudill, M., Zuttermeister, P. C., & Benson, H. (1991). An inventory of positive psychological attitudes with potential relevance to health outcomes: Validation and preliminary testing. *Behavioral Medicine, 17* (3), 121–129.

Kass, J. D., Friedman, R., Leserman, J., Zuttermeister, P. C., & Benson, H. (1991). Health outcomes and a new index of spiritual experience. *Journal of the Scientific Study of Religion, 30,* 203–211.

Kaufman, J. S., Jason, L. A., Sawlski, L. M., & Halpert, J. A. (1994). A comprehensive multi-media program to prevent smoking among black students. *Journal of Drug Education, 24,* 95–108.

Kellert, S. R., & Wilson, E. O. (Eds.). (1993). *The biophilia hypothesis.* Washington, DC: Island Press.

Kelly, J. G. (1977). The search for ideas and deeds that work. In G. W. Albee & J. M. Joffe (Eds.), *Primary prevention of psychopathology: Vol. 1. The Issues* (pp. 1–17). Hanover, NH: University of New England.

Kelly, J. G. (1985). The concept of primary prevention: Creating new paradigms. *Journal of Primary Prevention, 5,* 269–272.

Kelly, J. G. (1987, April). *Beyond prevention techniques: Generating social settings for a public's health.* Paper presented at the Tenth Erich Lindemann Memorial Lecture, Boston, MA.

Kelly, J. G. (1990). Changing contexts and the field of community psychology. *American Journal of Community Psychology, 18,* 769–792.

Kenny, J. (1991, September). *Gnosticism.* Paper presented at the Commons, Chicago, IL.

Kiecolt-Glaser, J. K., Garner, W., Speicher, C. E., Penn, G., & Glaser, R. (1984). Psychosocial modifiers of immunocompetence in medical students. *Psychosomatic Medicine, 46,* 7–14.

Kiecolt-Glaser, J. K., & Glaser, R. (1989). Psychoneuro-immunology: Past, present, and future. *Health Psychology, 8,* 677–682.

Kingry-Westergaard, C., & Kelly, J. G. (1990). A contextualist epistemology for ecological psychology. In P. Tolan, C. Keys, F. Chertok, & L. Jason (Eds.), *Researching community psychology: Issues of theory and methods* (pp. 23–31). Washington, DC: American Psychological Association.

Kitto, H.D.F. (1967). *The Greeks.* Baltimore, MD: Penguin.

Kobasa, S. C., Maddi, S., Puccetti, M. C., & Zola, M. A. (1985). Effectiveness of hardiness, exercise, and social support as resources against illness. *Journal of Psychosomatic Research, 29,* 525–533.

Kohlberg, L. (1981). *The philosophy of moral development.* San Francisco: Harper & Row.

Kohlberg, L., Ricks, D., & Snarey, J. (1984). Childhood development as a predictor of adaptation in adulthood. *Genetic Psychology Monographs, 110,* 91–172.

Kuhn, T. S. (1962). *The structure of scientific revolutions.* Chicago: University of Chicago Press.

Ladd, E. C. (1993/94). The myth of moral decline. *The Responsive Community, 4* (1), 52–68.

Laing, R. D. (1967). *The politics of experience.* New York: Pantheon.

Layne, C. (1989). Painful truths about depressives' cognitions. In J. M. Hooley, J. M. Neale, & G. C. Davison (Eds.), *Readings in abnormal psychology* (pp. 202–208). New York: John Wiley.

Lazarus, R. C. (1985). The trivialization of distress. In J. C. Rosen & L. J. Solomon (Eds.), *Prevention in health psychology* (pp. 279–298). Hanover, VT: University Press of New England.

Lerner, H. D., & Ehrlich, J. (1994). Psychoanalytic model. In V. B. Van Hasselt & M. Hersen (Eds.), *Advanced abnormal psychology* (pp. 67–91). New York: Plenum.

Lever, J. (1976). Sex differences in the games children play. *Social Problems, 23,* 478–487.

Levine, M., & Perkins, D. V. (1987). *Principles of community psychology: Perspectives and applications.* New York: Oxford University Press.

Levinson, D. J. (1978). *The seasons of a man's life.* New York: Alfred A. Knopf.

Lewin, K. (1951). *Field theory in social science.* New York: Harper & Row.

Linville, P. W. (1987). Self-complexity as a cognitive buffer against stress-related illness and depression. *Journal of Personality and Social Psychology, 52,* 663–676.

Livingston, J. C. (1989). *Anatomy of the sacred. An introduction to religion* (2nd ed.). New York: Macmillan.

Locke, S., & Colligan, D. (1987). *The healer within: The new medicine of mind and body.* New York: Mentor.

Lorenz, E. N. (1967). *The nature and theory of the general circulation of the atmosphere.* Geneva: World Meteorological Organization.

Lorenz, K. (1974). *On aggression.* (M. K. Wilson, Trans.). New York: Harcourt Brace Jovanovich.

Luks, A. (1992). *The healing power of doing good.* New York: Fawcett Columbine.

Lyon, L. (1989). *The community in urban society.* Lexington, MA: D. C. Heath.

Maddi, S. R. (1975). The existential neurosis. In D. L. Rosenhan & P. London (Eds.), *Theory and research in abnormal psychology* (pp. 126–143). New York: Holt, Rinehart, & Winston.

Mann, P. A. (1978). *Community psychology: Concepts and applications.* New York: The Free Press.

Mann, T. (1995). *The magic mountain: A novel.* (J. E. Woods, Trans.). New York: A. Knopf. (Originally published 1930.)

Maslow, A. (1962). *Toward a psychology of being.* Princeton, NJ: Van Nostrand.

May, R. (1960). *Existential psychology.* New York: Random House.

McCann, D. P. (1991). Hinduism. In J. D. Crossan (Ed.), *Religious worlds. Primary readings in comparative perspective* (pp. 13–68). Dubuque, IA: Kendall/Hunt.

McClelland, D. C. (1979). Inhibited power motivation and high blood pressure in men. *Journal of Abnormal Psychology, 88,* 182–190.

McKay, J. R. (1991). Assessing aspects of object relations associated with immune function: Development of the Affiliative Trust-Mistrust coding system. *Psychological Assessment, 3,* 641–647.

McLaughlin, C., & Davidson, G. (1985). *Builders of the dawn: Community lifestyles in a changing world.* Shutesbury, MA: Sirius.

McMillan, D. W., & Chavis, D. M. (1986). Sense of community: A definition and theory. *Journal of Community Psychology, 14,* 6–23.

McNamara, W. (1992). Psychology and the Christian mystical tradition. In C. T. Tart (Ed.), *Transpersonal psychologies* (pp. 367–408). New York: HarperCollins.

Melton, G. (1992). It's time for neighborhood research and action. *Child Abuse and Neglect, 16,* 909–913.

Merton, T. (1948). *The seven storey mountain.* New York: Harcourt Brace.

Meyer, R., & Haggarty, R. (1962). Streptococcal infections in families. *Pediatrics,* 539–549.

Meyrowitz, J. (1985). *No sense of place: The impact of electronic media on social behavior.* Oxford: Oxford University Press.

Mikulas, W. L. (1995). Conjunctive psychology: Issues of integration. *Journal of Psychotherapy Integration, 5,* 331–348.

Milgram, S. S. (1963). Behavioral study of obedience. *Journal of Abnormal and Social Psychology, 67,* 371–378.

Miller, A. B., & Keys, C. B. (1996). *The self-advocacy movement for persons with developmental disabilities: Principles of empowerment.* Manuscript submitted for publication.

Moen, P., Dempster-McClain, D., & Williams, R. M. (1989). Social integration and longevity: An event history analysis of women's roles and resilience. *American Sociological Review, 54,* 635–647.

Moos, R. H. (1984). Content and coping: Toward a unifying conceptual framework. *American Journal of Community Psychology, 12,* 5–25.

Morgan, A. E. (1942). *The small community.* Yellow Springs, OH: Community Service, Inc.

Morgan, M. (1994). *Mutant message down under.* New York: HarperCollins.

Murphy, H.B.M. (1980). Culture and schizophrenia. In I. Al-Issa (Ed.), *Culture and psychopathology* (pp. 221–249). Baltimore: University Park Press.

Murphy, H.B.M. (1983). *Comparative psychiatry.* Berlin: Springer-Verlag.

Murray, H. A. (1959). Beyond yesterday's idealism. Harvard Phi Betta Kappa address. In E. S. Shneidman (1981). *Endeavors in Psychology: Selections from the personology of Henry A. Miller.* New York: Harper.

Myeroff, B. (1978). *Number our days.* New York: Simon & Schuster.

National Advisory Mental Health Council. (1993). *Health care reform for Americans with severe mental illnesses.* Bethesda, MD: National Institute of Mental Health.

National Crime Survey (1991, 24 March). National crime survey preliminary press release. National Institute of Health.

The Needs Foundation. (1991). Brochure.

Neki, J. S. (1975). Sahaja: An Indian ideal of mental health. *Psychiatry, 38,* 1–10.

Nhat Hanh, T. (1991). *Old path white clouds: Walking in the footsteps of the Buddha.* Berkeley, CA: Parallax Press.

Nietzsche, F. W. (1964). *Complete works.* (Oscar Levy, trans. and ed.) New York: Russell and Russell.

Novick, P. (1995). Practicing holistic health. *Conscious Choice, March/April,* 44–45.

Ogintez, E. (1992, 23 July). Program meets needs of disabled, homeless. *Chicago Tribune,* pp. 1, 2.

O'Hanlon, D. J. (1981). Integration of spiritual practices: A western christian looks east. *The Journal of Transpersonal Psychology, 13* (2), 91–112.

Ornish, D. M. (1991). *Dr. Dean Ornish's program for reversing heart disease*. New York: Random House.

Ornstein, R. E. (1992). Contemporary Sufism. In C. T. Tart (Ed.), *Transpersonal psychologies: Perspectives on the mind from seven great spiritual traditions* (pp. 329–366). New York: HarperCollins.

Oster, G., Colditz, G. A., & Kelly, N. L. (1984). *The economic costs of smoking and benefits of quitting*. Lexington, MA: Lexington Books.

Orwell, G. (1950). *1984*. New York: New American Library.

Owens, C. M. (1992). Zen buddhism. In C. T. Tart (Ed.), *Transpersonal psychologies: Perspectives on the mind from seven great spiritual traditions* (pp. 155–202). New York: HarperCollins.

Pargament, K., & Maton, K. (in press). Religion in American life: A community psychology perspective. In J. Rappaport & E. Seidman (Eds.), *Handbook of Community Psychology*. New York: Wiley.

Parker, J. G., & Asher, S. R. (1987). Peer relations and later adjustment: Are low-accepted children at risk? *Psychological Bulletin, 102*, 357–389.

Patterson, J., & Kim, P. (1993/94). The decline and fall: An alarmed perspective. *The Responsive Community, 4* (1), 47–51.

Payne, I. R., Bergin, A. E., Bielema, K. A., & Jenkins, P. H. (1991). Review of religion and mental health: Prevention and the enhancement of psychosocial functioning. *Prevention in Human Services, 9* (2), 11–40.

Peck, M. S. (1987). *The different drum*. New York: Simon & Schuster.

Pennebaker, J. W. (1990). *Opening up: The healing power of confiding in others*. New York: William Morrow & Co.

Perls, F. S. (1973). *The Gestalt approach: Eye witness to therapy*. Palo Alto, CA: Science and Behavior Books.

Pert, C. B. (1986). The wisdom of receptors: Neuropeptides, the emotions, and bodymind. *Advances, 3*, (3), 8–16.

Plas, J. M., & Lewis, S. E. (1996). Environmental factors and sense of community in a planned town. *American Journal of Community Psychology, 24*, 109–143.

Purpel, D. E. (1989). *The moral and spiritual crisis in education: A curriculum for justice and compassion in education*. Granby, MA: Bergin & Garvey Publishers.

Putnam, R. D. (1993). *Making democracy work: Civic traditions in modern Italy*. Princeton, NJ: Princeton University Press.

Putnam, R. D. (1995, January). Bowling alone: America's declining social capital. *The Journal of Democracy, 6*, 65–68.

Rabb, T. K. (1993). *Renaissance lives: Portraits of an age*. New York: Pantheon Books.

Rappaport, J. (1981). In praise of paradox: A social policy of empowerment over prevention. *American Journal of Community Psychology, 9*, 1–25.

Read, K. A. (1991). Buddhism. In J. D. Crossan (Ed.), *Religious worlds: Primary readings in comparative perspective* (pp. 71–139). Dubuque, IA: Kendall/Hunt.

Redfield, J. (1994). *The celestine prophecy: An adventure*. New York: Warner Books.

Regier, D. A., Myers, J. K., Kramer, M., Robbins, L. N., Blazer, D. G., Hough, R. L., Eaton, W. W., & Locke, B. Z. (1984). The NIMA epidemiologic catchment area program: Historical context, major objectives, and study population characteristics. *Archives of General Psychiatry, 41,* 934–941.

Reich, W. (1948). *The function of the orgasm: Sex-economic problems of biological energy* (2nd ed.). (T. P. Wolfe, Trans.). New York: Orgone Institute Press.

Reynolds, D. K. (1980). *The quiet therapies: Japanese pathways to personal growth.* Honolulu: University of Hawaii Press.

Reynolds, D. K. (1984). *Playing ball on running water.* New York: Quill.

Rheingold, H. (1995). *The virtual community.* Reading, MA: Addison Wesley.

Rhodes, J. E., Contreras, J. M., & Mangelsdorf, S. C. (1994). Natural mentor relationships among Latina adolescent mothers: Psychological adjustment, moderating processes and the role of early parental acceptance. *American Journal of Community Psychology, 22,* 211–227.

Rhodes, J. E., & Jason, L. A. (1988). *Preventing substance abuse among children and adolescents.* New York: Pergamon Press.

Ring, K. (1984) *Heading toward omega: In search of the meaning of near-death experience.* New York: Morrow.

Rinpoche, S. (1993). *The Tibetan book of living and dying.* New York: HarperCollins.

Robbins, J. (1987). *Diet for a new America.* Walpole, NH: Stillpoint.

Rogers, C. R. (1957). The necessary and sufficient conditions of therapeutic personality change. *Journal of Consulting Psychology, 21,* 95–103.

Robinson, W. L., Watkins-Ferrell, P., Davis-Scott, P., & Ruch-Ross, H. (1993). Preventing teenage pregnancy. In D. S. Glenwick & L. A. Jason (Eds.), *Promoting health and mental health in children, youth, and families* (pp. 99–124). New York: Springer Publishing Co.

Romer, J. (1988). *Testament, the Bible and history.* New York: Holt.

Rothenbuhler, E. W. (1991). The process of community involvement. *Communication Monographs, 58,* 63–78.

Rubin, L. (1976). *Worlds of pain.* New York: Basic Books.

Sahtoris, E. (1989). *Gaia: The human journey from chaos to cosmos.* New York: Pocket Books.

Salina, D., Jason, L. A., Hedeker, D., Kaufman, J., Lesondak, L., Taylor, S., & Kimball, P. (1994). A follow-up of a media-based, worksite smoking cessation program. *American Journal of Community Psychology, 22,* 257–271.

Sarason, S. B. (1972). *The culture of the school and the problem of change.* Boston: Allyn & Bacon.

Sarason, S. B. (1974). *The psychological sense of community: Prospects for a community psychology.* San Francisco: Jossey-Bass.

Sarason, S. B., Carroll, C., Maton, K., Cohen, S., & Lorentz, E. (1977). *Human services and resource networks.* San Francisco: Jossey-Bass.

Sarason, S. B., & Klaber, M. (1985). The school as a social situation. In M. R. Rosenzweig & L. W. Porter (Eds.), *Annual Review of Psychology* (pp. 115–140). Palo Alto, CA: Annual Review Inc.

Saraswati, S. S. (1984). *Kundalini Tantra.* Behar, India: Sri G. K. Kejriwal.

Sartre, J. P. (1947). *No exit (Huis clos), a play in one act, and the flies (Les mouches), a play in three acts* (Stuart Gilbert, Trans.). New York: Knopf.

Sartre, J. P. (1956). *Being and nothingness* (H. E. Barnes, Trans.). New York: Simon & Schuster.

Schlesinger, Jr., A. M. (1992). *The disuniting of America.* New York: Norton.

Schmid, R. F. (1987). *Traditional foods are your best medicine.* New York: Ballantine Books.

Schwartz, G. E. (1990). Psychobiology of repression and health: A systems approach. In J. L. Singer (Ed.), *Repression and dissociation: Implications for personality theory, psychopathology, and health.* Chicago: University of Chicago Press.

Schwartz, T. (1995). *What really matters. Searching for wisdom in America.* New York: Bantam.

Shaffer, C. R., & Anundsen, K. (1993). *Creating community anywhere: Finding support and connection in a fragmented world.* New York: G. P. Putnam's Sons.

Shapiro, D. (1989). Judaism as a journey of transformation: Consciousness, behavior, and society. *Journal of Transpersonal Psychology, 21* (1), 13–59.

Slama, J. (1993). Missing information. *Conscious Choice, 6* (2), 4.

Smith, M. B. (1994). Selfhood at risk: Postmodern perils and the perils of postmodernism. *American Psychology, 49,* 405–411.

Some, M. P. (1995). *Of water and the spirit. Ritual, magic and initiation in the life of an African Shaman.* New York: Penguin.

Spiegel, D. (1991). A psychosocial intervention and survival time of patients with metastatic breast cancer. *Advances, 7,* 10–19.

Spilka, B., Hood, R. W., Jr., & Gorsuch, R. L. (1985). *The psychology of religion: An empirical approach.* Englewood Cliffs, NJ: Prentice-Hall.

Spretnak, C. (1991). *States of grace.* New York: HarperCollins.

Statser, C. (1978). *Chopping wood, carrying water.* Oatman, AZ: Padma Press.

Staudinger, U. M., Smith, J., & Baltes, P. B. (1992). Wisdom-related knowledge in a life review task: Age differences and the role of professional specialization. *Psychology and Aging, 7,* 271–281.

Stein, M. R. (1960). *The eclipse of community.* New York: Harper Torchbook.

Stone, M. (1976). *When God was a woman.* San Diego: Harest/HBJ.

Sundberg, N. D. (1985). The use of future studies in training for prevention and promotion in mental health. *The Journal of Primary Prevention, 6* (2), 98–114.

Swift, W. B. (1995). The kindness cure. *New Age Journal* (September-October), 84–87, 154–157.

Taubes, G. (1990). The body chaotic. *Discover, 11,* 49–53.

Thomas, L. E., & Cooper, P. E. (1978). Measurement and incidence of mystical experiences: An exploratory study. *Journal for the Scientific Study of Religion, 17* (4), 433–437.

Thompson, D. W. & Jason, L. A. (1988). Street gangs and preventive interventions. *Criminal Justice and Behavior, 15,* 323–333.

Tornatzky, L. G., & Fergus, E. O. (1982). Innovation and diffusion in mental health: The Community Lodge. In A. M. Jeger & R. Slotnick (Eds.), *Community mental health: A behavior-ecological perspective* (pp. 113–126). New York: Plenum.

Trickett, E. J., Kelly, J. G., & Vincent, T. (1985). The spirit of ecological inquiry in community research. In E. Susskind & D. Klein (Eds.), *Community research: Methods, paradigms, and applications* (pp. 5–38). New York: Praeger.

Tryon, W. W. (1995). Neural networks for behavior therapists: What they are and why they are important. *Behavior Therapy, 26,* 295–318.

Upshur, J.H.L., Terry, J. J., Holoka, J. P., Goff, R. D., & Lowry, B. (1991). *World history* (Vol. 2). New York: West.

U.S. Bureau of the Census. (1986). *Money, income, and poverty status of families and persons in the U.S.: 1986* (Current population report, No. 157). Washington, DC: U.S. Government Printing Office.

Vaughan, F. (1979). Transpersonal psychotherapy: Context, content, and process. *Journal of Transpersonal Psychology, 11* (2), 101–110.

Walsh, R. N. (1990). *The spirit of shamanism*. Los Angeles, CA: J. P. Tarcher.

Watts, R. J., & Abdul-Adil, J. (1994). Psychological aspects of oppression and sociopolitical development. In R. Newby & T. Manley (Eds.), *The poverty of inclusion, innovation and interventions: The dilemma of the African-American underclass*. Rutgers, NJ: Rutgers University Press.

Webster, K. (1990, November/December). The case against Swami Rama of the Himalayas. *The Yoga Journal*, 58–69, 92–94.

Wegela, K. K. (1988). "Touch and go" in clinical practice: Some implications of the view of intrinsic health for psychotherapy. *Journal of Contemplative Psychotherapy, 5*, 3–23.

Weide, T. N. (1973). Varieties of transpersonal therapy. *Journal of Transpersonal Psychology, 5* (1), 7–14.

Wilber, K. (1995). *Sex, ecology, spirituality: The spirit of evolution*. Boston: Shambhala.

Winett, R. A. (1993). Media-based behavior change approaches for prevention. In D. S. Glenwick & L. A. Jason (Eds.), *Promoting health and mental health in children, youth, and families* (pp. 181–204). New York: Springer.

Wood, M. (1992, February) Legacy. Public Broadcasting System telecast, 3 February 1992.

Wurtele, S. K. (1993). Prevention of child physical and sexual abuse. In D. S. Glenwick & L. A. Jason (Eds.), *Promoting health and mental health in children, youth, and families*. (pp. 33–50). New York: Springer.

Yankelovich, D. (1993/94). The return to pragmatism. *The Responsive Community, 4* (1), 30–39.

Zigler, E., & Finn, M. (1982). A vision of child care in the 1980s. In L. A. Bond & J. M. Joffe (Eds.), *Facilitating infant and early childhood development* (pp. 443–465). Hanover, VT: University Press of New England.

Zukav, Gary. (1989). *The seat of the soul*. New York: Simon & Schuster.

Index

Abdul-Adil, J., 29
Access, stage of Buddhism, 60
Adam and Eve, 14, 15, 118
Adams, R. E., 70
Adaptation, ecological principle of, 124
Addams, Jane, 77
Adelman, M. B., 82
Ader, R., 35
Adler, A., 41, 42
Adolescence, modern problems of, 2
Affiliative trust, 49
African religions, 67, 68
Age of reason, 20
Aggression, 8, 9
Agriculture, 11
AIDS, 1, 82; prevention of, 99
Al-Islam, 65, 66
Allah, 65
Albee, G. W., 3, 102
Alcoholics Anonymous (A. A.), 79
Alexian Brothers, 82
Alinsky, S., 123
Allison, Bill, 78
Allport, G. W., 54
Amate Collegiate House, 83
American Association for Protecting Children, 2
American Lung Association, 94, 95
Amish community, 75
Anderson, S., 69
Anes, M. D., 105, 106
Animal ancestry, 8
Antibiotics, 3
Antisocial, stage of spiritual development, 55
Antonovsky, A., 121
Arrien, A., 5
Aryans, 14, 117
Asceticism, 64
Asher, S. R., 2
Assagioli, R., 49

Bacon, Sir Francis, 16
Baltes, P. B., 53
Baltes, Paul, 122
Banks, C., 10
Barker, R. G., 103
Barnes, Hazel, 18
Bartel, N. R., 121
Batson, C. D., 54
Baumeister, R. F., 72

Belief systems, 5
Bellah, R. N., 4, 26, 46
Bell's theorem, 34
Benedict, Ruth, 20
Bennetto, L., 97
Benson, H., 38, 121, 123
Bergin, A. E., 54
Berk, M., 106
Berry, T., 55–56
Bhakti yoga, 59
Biderman, M., 123
Bielema, K. A., 54
Biglan, A., 90
Bill of Rights, 90
Billows, W., 78
Binah, 62
Biophilia, Edmond Wilson's concept of, 18
Birkhead, S. H., 106
Bishop, P., 72
Blank, W., 62
Blumenkrantz, D. G., 30
Body therapies, 68
Bonaventure House, 82
Borysenko, J., 38, 49
Bower, B., 36
Bradshaw, J., 41
Brave New World, 50
Breakdown, phase of social change, 112
Brecht, M., 120
Briggs, Beatrice, 52
Briggs, J., 34
Brim, Gilbert, 122
Brooke, T., 60
Bry, B. H., 32
Buckenberger, L., 94
Buckner, J. C., 124
Buddha, 44, 60, 61, 117
Buddhism, 31, 49, 60, 61, 118; access stage of, 60; *Jhana* stage of, 60; Mahayana school, 60; *Nirodh*, 60; Nirvana, 60; Therevada school, 60
Buddhists, 33, 50, 108; aspects of health, 55; Four Noble Truths of, 61; Hinayana, 39; Mahayana, 60; Therevada, 60; Zen, 60
BUILD (Chicago), 84
Bureaucratization, 20
Burkhardt, M. A., 55, 56
Buss, D. M., 9, 115

Camara, Dom Helder, 68
Campbell, J., 11–13, 16, 22, 39, 40, 43–45, 58, 60, 116
Camphill, 85
Camus, 18
Cannon, W., 35
Carroll, C., 103
Catholicism, rise of, 118
Cavalieri, P., 8
The Celestine Prophecy, 38
Chakras, 62, 68
Chamberlin, J., 85
Chaos, stage of community building, 73
Chaos theory, 34
Chaotic, stage of spiritual development, 55
Chavis, D. M., 123, 124
Chertok, F., 72, 124
Chicago Defender, 95, 96
Chicago Tribune, 97, 99
Chi energy, 68
Child passenger restraint, 92; Association, 92; Bill, 92
Chodorow, N., 21
Chopping Wood, Carrying Water, 69
Chopra, D., 36, 37
Christ, 44
Christianity, 63–65
Christian mysticism, 63, 64
Cigarette sales to minors, 104–106
Civic engagement, networks of, 73
Clarity, aspect of health, 55, 56
Clean water, 2
Coditz, G. A., 95
Co-housing, 83
Cohen, N., 35
Cohen, S., 35, 103
Collaboration, between psychologists and communities, 89–100, 103, 104
Colligan, D., 35, 36
Communal, stage of spiritual development, 55

Communion, Berry's pattern of the universe, 55, 56
Communitarian: model, 90; movement, 164
Community: alliances, 99, 100; building, 73, 74, 80, 83–86; effort, 89; input, 89; intentional, 83; ownership, 89; stage of community building, 74
Community psychologists, 75, 80, 89, 90, 102, 103, 106, 107
Community psychology, 89, 102, 103, 106, 107
Competence-building approach, 103
Computers, 51
Confucius, 117
Consciousness, The Evolution of, 11
Constantine, Emperor, 118
Contextualism, 32
Contextual model, 121
Contreras, J. M., 84
Cook, T. D., 102
Cooper, P. E., 54
Copernicus, 17, 33, 121
Cordovero, Moses, 63
Cornford, F. M., 25, 28
Cosmological, function of myths, 39, 40
Cotter, P. R., 72
Cottrell, L., 74
Cousins, N., 35
Cowan, J., 84
Crawford, I., 99
Crawford-Mason, C., 26
Crime, 1
Critique of Practical Reason, 121
Crystallized intelligence, 54
Csikszentmihalyi, M., 47, 48, 60
Cultural intolerance: of ambiguity, 112; of chronic social issues, 112; of suffering, 112
Cultural relativity, 121
Curran, T., 98
Cycling of resources, ecological principle of, 124

Dalai Lama, 61
Darwin, 17
Davidson, G., 19, 74
Davidson, W. B., 72
Deconstructive postmodernism, 32, 33, 121
DeKay, W. T., 9, 115
Delancey Street Foundation, 81
Dempster-McClain, D., 72
DePaul University, 80, 83, 95
Derrida, Jacques, 32
Descartes, 16
Development, midlife, 122
Dewey, John, 27
Diener, C., 7
Diener, E., 7
Diet, contemporary, 2
Differentiation, Berry's pattern of the universe, 55, 56
Divorce, 2
Dobyne, L., 26
Domestic violence, 1, 2
Doniger, W., 39
Doolittle, R. J., 124
Dreher, H., 9, 37
Dropout, rates of, 2
Drug abuse, 2; prevention programs, 97, 98, 104
Dualism, 13, 15
Duality, 13, 15; psyche-soma, 112; subject-object, 57
Duany, 82
Duffy, K. G., 102
Dugger, R., 2, 101
Dunham, H. W., 123
Dunne, J., 78
Dvorchak, P. A., 79

Eastern religions, 39; similarities with Christian religions, 64. *See also names of specific religions*
Ecological: model/paradigm, 103; perspective, 102, 108; principles, 124
Ecological postmodernism, 33
Ecological post-modernists, 121
Ecosystem, 2
Eco-transformational: interventions, 108, 111–114; model, 106–109
Education, 26–32
Ehrlich, J., 41
Eightfold Noble Path, 61

Einstein, 33, 34
Eliade, Mircea, 39
Ellison, C. W., 123
Emergency, phase of social change, 112
Emotional intelligence, 27
Empowerment, 103; model, 108
Emptiness, stage of community building, 73
Energy crises, 51
Energy systems, in the body, 68
Epstein, I., 61–63
Equipoise, Samadhi, 58
Erikson, E. H., 45
Etzioni, A., 2, 75, 90, 91
Evans, A. S., 35
Evolutionary psychology, 115
The Evolution of Consciousness, 11
Existential: frustration, 47; neurosis, 47; phase of social change, 112
Existentialism, 47
Existentialists, 18, 47, 52
External symbols, loss of, 17, 18

Fairweather, G., 76
Faith, Five Pillars of, 65
Families InTouch: Understanding AIDS, 99
Family Resource Coalition, 85
Fawcett, S. B., 90, 93
Featherman, David, 122
Federal Anti-Drug Abuse Act of 1988, 79
Fennell, P. A., 111–114
Fergus, E. O., 76
Ferrari, J. R., 78, 80
Finn, M., 2
Five Pillars of Faith, 65
Flay, B., 95
The Flies, 18
Flow, 47
Flow states, 47
Fluid intelligence, 53, 54
Formal, stage of spiritual development, 55
Fortes, Meyer, 20
Foundational values, 108, 109, 121
Foundational Values Scale, 56, 57
Foundation for Community Encouragement, 85
Four Noble Truths, 61
Four-Phase Model of Social Change, 112–114
Fowler, J. W., 55
Fox, D. R., 4
Frankl, V. E., 47
Freedom, Samadhi, 58
Freud, S., 8, 21, 41, 42
Frey, L. R., 82
Friedman, R., 121, 123
Friere, Paulo, 27, 68
Fuller, Buckminister, 50
Functional, theory of myths, 39
Furman, F. K., 118

Gaines, S. O., 67
Galileo, 121
Gallagher, W., 122
Gandhi, 28
Gang activity, 1, 2
Gannett Outdoors, 96
Garner, W., 35
Gavazze, S. M., 30
Gelernter, C. Q., 80
Gemeinschaft, 19, 123
Gender differences, 115
Genocide, 9
Gerber, R., 34
Gesellschaft, 19, 20
Gestalt therapy, 48
Gesten, E. L., 102
Gesundheit Institute, 85
Gevurah, 62
Gilbert, A., 117
Gilligan, C., 21, 39
Glaser, R., 35
Glynn, T. J., 123, 124
Gnostic(s), 31; texts, 63, 64
Goddess, 11, 12, 14 –16; traditions, 108
Goff, R. D., 11, 13, 19
Goldman, D., 27
Goleman, D., 37, 60
Goodall, Jane, 8, 9
Goodman, D., 94, 98
Gorsuch, R. L., 54, 55

Gould Farm, 85
Goyeche, J. R. M., 59
Grams, G., 79
Granada, Moses de Leon of, 62
Grandmother's House, 85
Grassroots organizations, 99
Graves, R., 14
Greeley, A. M., 53, 54
Greenhouse effect, 3
Greiner, B., 98
Gruder, C. L., 93
Gruder, Larry, 37
Gurin, J., 37
Guskin, S. L., 121
Gutierrez, Gustavo, 68

Habits of the Heart, 4
Haggarty, R., 35
Hakomi body-centered psychotherapy, 48–49
Hall, J. R., 123
Halpert, J. A., 95
Hanaway, E. K., 2
Hanna, F. J., 50
Harmonious interconnectedness, Burkhardt's characteristic of spirituality, 56
Harmony: component of Foundational Values Scale, 56; *samadhi*, 58
Hasidic Judaism, 63
Hatha yoga, 59
Hay, D., 54
Hay, L. L., 49
Hayes, J. W., 121
Healing, process of, 113, 114
Heinze, R. I., 67
Heney, C., 10
Henry, Prince of Portugal, 119
Hermetics, 64
The Hero with a Thousand Faces, 40
Hertz, J. H., 118
Hesed, 62
"High Top Tower" series, 97, 98
Hinayana, school of Buddhism, 39, 60
Hinduism, 31, 57, 58, 117, 118
Hirsch, B. J., 32
HIV, 82; prevention of, 99
Hobfoll, S., 90
Hod, 62
Hoff, Benjamin, 7
Hogge, J. H., 124
Hokhman, 62
Holoka, J. P., 11, 13, 19
Holy Grail, 40
Holy Spirit, energy of, 68
HOME (Housing Opportunities and Maintenance for the Elderly), 77
Homelessness, 1, 2
Homer, 43
Homo erectus, 10, 116
Homo habilis, 10, 115
Homo sapiens, 10, 11
Hood, R. W., Jr., 54, 55, 122, 123
Hope, A., 27
Hopkins, P., 69
Horney, K., 41
Houston, J., 38
Hull House, 77
Humanistic psychology, 47; therapies, 48
Human Kindness Foundation, 81
Human sacrifice, 116
Huss, Jan, 120
Hutterite sect, 74
Huxley, A., 50

Ida, 58, 59
Illinois Child Passenger Restraint Law, 92, 93
Illinois Department of Alcohol and Substance Abuse (DASA), 97
Illumination: christian mystics' life phase of, 64; *samadhi*, 58
Imani, 68
Independence, 109
Index of Core Spiritual Experience, 123
Individual, stage of spiritual development, 55
Industrialization, 20; problems associated with, 101
Industrial Revolution, 19, 20, 26
Information Age, 4, 5, 26
Inner strength, Burkhardt's characteristic of spirituality, 56
Innisfree Village, 85

Institutional, stage of spiritual development, 55
Integration, phase of social change, 112
Intelligence, 56; crystallized, 54; emotional, 27; fluid, 53, 54
Intentional communities, 83
Interconnectedness, 56, 109
Interdependence, ecological principle of, 124
Isabella, Queen of Spain, 119
Islam, 65, 66
Italy, historical analysis of politics of, 118, 119

James, William, 54, 122
Janists, 39
Jason et al., 2, 29, 56, 80
Jason, L. A., 29, 35, 72, 75, 78, 79, 84, 91–95, 97, 98, 102, 104–106, 111, 113, 114
Jenkins, P. H., 54
Jewish mysticism, 61, 62
Jhana, 60
Ji, P. Y., 105, 106
Jnana yoga, 59
Johanson, Donald, 10, 115
Johanson, G., 49
Johnson, S., 98
Joyce, James, 44
Judaism, 61–63, 118
Jung, 39, 42, 43, 64

Kabat-Zinn, J., 36
Kabbalah, 62–63
Kant, Immanual, 121
Karenga, Maulana, 68
Karma yoga, 59
Kasl, S. V., 35
Kass, J. D., 121, 123
Kaufman, J. S., 95
Kellert, S. R., 18
Kelly, J. G., 32, 103, 124
Kelly, N. L., 95
Kenny, J., 63, 64
Kepler, 121
Kessler, R., 122
Kessler, S., 31
Keys, C. B., 85
Kids InTouch, 97
Kiecolt-Glaser, J. K., 35
Kindness House, 81, 82
King, Jr., Martin Luther, 28
Kingry-Westergaard, C., 32, 103
Kirkwood, John, 93
Kitto, H. D. F., 28
Klaber, M., 27
Klich, M., 93
Knowledge, wisdom-related, 122
Kobasa, S. C., 36
Kobayashi, R. B., 75
Kohlberg, L., 21, 27, 55
Kohut, H., 41
Kuhn, Thomas, 33
Kujichagulia, 68
Kundalini: energy, 68; yoga, 59
Kundalini Tantra, 59
Kurtz, R., 48, 49
Kuumba, 68
Kwanzaa, 68

Lachman, M., 122
Ladd, E. C., 7, 121
Lahmar, K., 97
Laing, R. D., 42
Lao Tsu, 117
l'Arche ("the Arch"), 77, 78
Lattimore, B., 84
Layne, C., 46
Lazarus, R. C., 46
Leach, E. R., 20
Leakey, Mary, 115
Leary, M. R., 72
Le Chambon, 74
Legislation: cigarette sales to minors, 105, 106; initiatives, 102; research to enact, 91–93
Lerner, H. D., 41
Leserman, J., 121, 123
Lever, J., 22
Levine, M., 2
Levinson, D. J., 21
Levi-Strauss, Claude, 39

Lewin, K., 103
Lewis, S. E., 83
Liberation theology, 68
Linville, P. W., 42
Lipset, S. M., 121
Livingston, J. C., 11, 12, 39, 116
Locke, S., 35, 36
Lodge, The, 76, 77
Logical positivism, 32, 33
Logotherapy, Victor Frankl's, 47
Lorentz, E., 103
Lorenz, E. N., 34
Lorenz, K., 8
Lowry, B., 11, 13, 19
Lozoff, Bo and Sita, 81, 82
Luks, A., 72
Lung Association, Chicago, 93, 94, 96, 98–100
Luria, Rabbi Issac, 63
Luther, Martin, 120
Lyme disease, 3
Lyon, L., 19, 71, 123

MacArthur Foundation Research Network on Successful Midlife Development, 121
MacDonald, D., 124
Machiavelli, 120
Maddi, S. R., 36, 47
Madsen, R., 4, 26
Mahayana, school of Buddhism, 60
Malinowski, Bronislaw, 39
Malkhut, 62
Mangelsdorf, S. C., 84
Mann, P. A., 103
Mann, T., 43
Mantra yoga, 59
Marriage, 2, 44
Mask, as persona, 42
Maslow, A., 47
Matese, F. J., 91
Maton, K., 54, 103
May, R., 47
Maya, 44
Mayan civilization, 117
McCann, D. P., 28, 118
McClelland, D. C., 22
McKay, J. R., 49
McLaughlin, C., 19, 74
McMillan, D. W., 123, 124
McMahon, S. D., 95
McNamara, W., 64
Meaning in life, Burkhardt's characteristic of spirituality, 56
Media-based health-promotion interventions, 93–99
Melton, G., 75
Mental Patients' Liberation Front (MPLF), 85
Merton, T., 64, 65
Mesopotamia, 13
Metaphysical: function of myths, 40; journeys, 44, 45
Meyer, R., 35
Midlife development, 122
Mikulas, W. L., 49
Milgram, Stanley, 10
Miller, A. B., 85
Mission, psychological sense of community factor, 72
Moen, P., 72
Molloy, P., 78 80
Monotheism, 118
Moos, R. H., 103
Moral values, schools' role in teaching, 90
Morgan, A. E., 19
Morisy, A., 54
Morita therapy, 48
Moses de Leon of Granada, 62
Motor vehicle accidents, 92, 93
Motoyama, Hiroshi, 59
Muhammed, the prophet, 65
Muktananda, 70
Murphy, H. B. M., 74
Murray, H. A., 1
Muslims, 65, 66
Mutant Message, 38
Mysteries, The, 31
Mystical: experiences in religions, 68; stage of spiritual development, 55
Mysticism Scale, 123

Mythology, 38–45, 107; personal, 31
Myths, theories of, 39, 40; cosmological function of, 39, 40; metaphysical function of, 40; psychological function of, 40; recreation of, 107; sociological function of, 40

Nadis, 58, 59
Nanotechnololgy, 52
National Conference of Adopters Coalition for Community Living, 76
Native American(s), 24, 31, 33, 39; balance with nature, 57, 108; democracy, 90
Native American spirituality, 66, 67
Nature: component of Foundational Values Scale, 56; control of, 117, 118; need to be in balance with, 12, 13, 117
Naylor, K., 98
Nazis, 9
Neanderthals, 10, 116
Needs Foundation, 78
Neki, J. S., 57
New Age: movements, 69, 70; religions, 69, 70
Newbrough, J. R., 32
New Testament, 26
Newtonian physics, 33
Nezah, 62
Nguzo Saba, 68
Nhat Hanh, Thich, 25, 61
Nia, 68
Niederman, J. C., 35
Nielsen ratings, 94
Nietzsche, 43
Nineteen Eighty-Four (1984), 50
Nirodh, 60
Nirvana, 60
Nonlinear dynamics, 34
Novick, P., 38
Nutrition intervention, 98, 99

Odysseus, 43
Ogintez, E., 78
O'Hanlon, D. J., 64
Old Path White Clouds, 25
Old Testament, 14, 15, 26
On Aggression, 8
Operation Snowball, 104
Orestes, 18
Ornish, D. M., 37
Ornstein, R. E., 11, 66
Orwell, George, 50
Oster, G., 95
Ottens, A. J., 50
Oxford group, 79
Oxford House, 78–81

Paradise myth, 14
Pargament, K., 54
Parker, J. G., 2
Pascal, 17
Payne, I. R., 54
Peak experiences, 47
Peat, F. D., 34
Peck, M. S., 55, 73, 85
Penn, G., 35
Pennebaker, J. W., 41
People First of Illinois, 85
Perkins, D. V., 2
Perls, F. S., 48
Pert, C., 35
Phenomenological, theory of myths, 39
Philip II, King of Spain, 120
Philosophical systems, 32, 33
Physical sciences, 33–35
Physics, 33–35
Piaget, J., 55
Pingala, 58, 59
Plas, J. M., 83
Plater-Dyberk, 82
Plato, 25, 28; Plato's cave, 25; *The Republic of Plato*, 28
P'nai Or, 63
Pokorny, S. B., 97
Pooper-scooper intervention, 91, 92
Pope Innocent III, 63
Post-modern deconstructive model, 121
Prana, 58, 59
Pregnancy, adolescent, 2
Prevention strategies, primary, 102
Prison-Ashram Project, 82
Protestant work ethic, 121

Prudential Insurance Company, 93, 94, 98, 100
Pseudo-community, stage of community building, 73
Psyche-soma duality, 112
Psychoanalytic: theory, 8, 21, 39, 41, 42; theory of myths, 39
Psychological, function of myths, 40
Psychological sense of community, 71–75, 123, 124; breakdown in, 101, 107, 122, 123. *See also* Sense of community
The Psychological Sense of Community, 71
Psychoneuroimmunology, 35, 36
Psychotherapy, 46–50. *See also names of specific therapies*
Puccetti, M. C., 36
Purification, Christian mystic's life phase of, 64
Purpel, D. E., 27, 28
Putnam, R. D., 73, 101, 117, 118

Quantum Healing, 36, 37
Quantum Healing: Exploring the Frontiers of Mind/Body Medicine, 36
Quran, 65

Rabb, T. K., 119
Radin, Paul, 20
Raja yoga, 59
Rajneesh, Bhagwan Shree, 70
Rama, Swami, 69
Rappaport, J., 103
Read, K. A., 118
Reciprocal responsibility, 75; psychological sense of community factor, 73
Reciprocity, norms of, 73
Reed, E. S., 67
REEM (Religious Experience Episodes Measure), 122, 123
Regier et al., 1
Reich, Wilhelm, 68
Reichler, A., 56
Reischl, T. M., 32
Religion, functions of, 54
Religious Experience Episodes Measure (REEM), 122, 123
Religious settings, community building in, 84, 84
Renaissance, 16, 119, 120
Renaissance Lives: Portraits of an Age, 119
The Republic of Plato, 28
Restabilization, phase of social change, 112
Reynolds, D. K., 48
Rheingold, H., 51
Rhodes, J. E., 84, 104
Ricks, D., 27
Riders of the Cosmic Circuit, 70
Ring, K., 55
Rinpoche, Sogyal, 101
Rite of Passage Experience (ROPE), 30
Rites of passage, 30, 31, 39, 107
Rituals, 30, 31, 107
Robbins, J., 3
Robinson et al., 2
Rogers, C. R., 48
Roman Catholic Church, 120
Romer, J., 17
Rose, T., 92
Ross, J. M., 54
Rubin, L., 22

Safed mystics, 63
Sahtoris, E., 109
Saint Thomas, 44
Salina, D., 95
Salmon, Michael and Lilo, 77
Samadhi, 58
Sarason, S. B., 27, 71, 72, 103
Saraswati, S. S., 59
Sartre, J. P., 18
Sawlski, L. M., 95
Schlesinger, Jr., A. M., 23
Schmid, R. F., 2
Schnopp-Wyatt, D. L., 106
Schwartz, G. E., 41
Schwartz, T., 69, 70
Science, the rise of, 16, 17, 112, 120, 121
Scientific method, 107
Seaside, Florida, 82, 83

The Seat of the Soul, 89
Seekins, T., 93
Sefiroth, 62
Segundo, Juan Luis, 68
Self-help approach, to build sense of community, 123
Sense of coherence, Antonovsky's concept, 121
Sense of community, 71–87; rebuilding, 108, 123. *See also* Psychological sense of community
Sense of meaning in life, Burkhardt's characteristic of spirituality, 56
Separation from nature, 10–17, 112
Sephirah, 62
Sephirot, 62
Sexual activity, adolescent, 2
Shadish, W. R., 102
Shadow, 41 43, 111
Shamanism, 66, 67
Shamans, 66, 67
Shapiro, D., 63
Shreeve, J., 10, 115
Simple Living, 86
Singer, P., 8
Sir Galahad, 40
Sisyphus, 18
Skeptic, stage of spiritual development, 55
Slama, J., 4
Smith, J., 53
Smith, M., 98
Smoking: cessation interventions, 93, 94, 99; prevention, 95–97. *See also* Woodridge Project
Smoking Deserves a Smart Answer, 95
Snarey, J., 27
Social capital, 73
Social change, four-phase model of, 112–114
Social competence approach, 103; limitations of, 108
Social context/framework, 111, 112, 124
Social exchange system, 11
Social interventions, 108
Sociological, function of myths, 40
Sociologists, 29
Sociopolitical development, five stages of, 29
Socrates, 28
Some, M. P., 67
Spaciousness, Buddhist aspect of health, 55, 56
Speicher, C. E., 35
Spiegel, D., 38
Spilka, B., 54, 55
Spinoza, 63
Spiritual: experience, 55, 56; Index of Core Spiritual Experience, 123; stages of development, 55; traditions, 57
Spirituality, 54, 57, 109; component of Foundational Values Scale, 56
Spiritual Well-Being Scale, 123
Spontaneity, *samadhi*, 58
Spretnak, C., 12–15, 33, 53, 60, 61, 66, 108
States of Grace, 53
Statser, C., 68
Staudinger, U. M., 53
Stein, D., 93
Stein, M. R., 20
Stone, M., 12, 14
Stress-management intervention, 98
Structural, interpretations of myths, 39
The Structure of Scientific Revolutions, 33
Stuart, E. N., 38
Subjectivity, Berry's pattern of the universe, 55, 56
Substance abuse, 2; prevention programs, 97, 98, 104
Succession, ecological principle of, 124
Success Over Stress, 98
Suffering, and process of healing, 113
Sufi mission, 66
Sufism, 66
Sullivan, W. M., 4, 26
Sundberg, N. D., 5
Sushumna, 58
Swidler, A., 4, 26
Swindle, R. W., 32

Synar Amendment, 106
System-wide interventions, 104

Tait, E., 94
Talbot, Officer B., 105, 106
Taoism, 117
The Tao of Pooh, 7
Tate, L., 79
Taubes, G., 34
Technical assistance, approach to building sense of community, 123
Technology, 50–52
Terry, J. J., 11, 13, 19
Therapy, 46–50. *See also names of specific therapies*
Therevada, school of Buddhism, 60
Thomas, L. E., 54
The Tibetan Book of Living and Dying, 101
Tiferet, 62
Timmel, S., 27
Tipton, S. M., 4, 26
Tobacco Licensing and Enforcement Law, 105
Tonga Islands, 74
Topsoil, depletion of, 2, 3
Torah, 61, 62
Tornatzky, L. G., 76
Transpersonal therapies, 49
Trickett, E. J., 103
True Value Hardware, 94, 98, 100
Truths, Four Noble, 61
Tryon, W. W., 51

Ujamaa, 68
Ujima, 68
Ummah, 65
Umoja, 68
Union, Christian mystic's life phase of, 64
Upanishads, 58, 117
Upshur, J.-H. L., 11, 13, 19, 61
Urbanization, 20

Values: crisis of, 107; foundational, 108, 109
Van Egeren, L., 98
Vanier, Jean, 77, 78
Vaughan, F., 49
Vedas, 58
Ventis, W. L., 54
Vincent, T., 103
The Virtual Community, 51

Walsh, R. N., 67
Wandersman, A., 124
Warmth: aspect of health, 55; component of Foundational Values Scale, 56
Watson, P. J., 123
Watts, R., 29
Webster, K., 70
Wegela, K. K., 55, 56
Weide, T. N., 49
Weight reduction intervention, 98, 99
Western religions, 39; ethics from, 108. *See also names of specific religions*
What Really Matters: Searching for Wisdom in America, 69
Wilber, K., 10–12, 116
Williams, R. M., 72
Williamson, G. M., 35
Wilson, E., 18
Winett, R. A., 90
Wisdom, 53, 56, 69; as measured by Foundational Values Scale, 56
Wisdom-related knowledge, 122
Wisdom traditions, 69, 101–109, 112, 113
Wong, F. Y., 102
Wood, M., 13
Woodridge Project, 104–106
Workplaces, community building in, 84
Wurtele, S. K., 2

Xaverious, P., 105

Yesod, 62
Yoga, 59; Bhakti, 59; Hatha, 59; Jnana, 59; Karma, 59; Kundalini, 59; Mantra, 59; Raja, 59

Zen, school of Buddhism, 60; masters, 69

Zigler, E., 2
Zimbardo, Phillip, 10
Zohar, 62–63
Zola, M. A., 36
Zolik, E. S., 91, 92
Zoroaster, 14
Zukav, G., 89
Zuttermeister, P. C., 121, 123

About the Author and Contributors

LEONARD A. JASON is a Professor of Psychology at DePaul University. He received his Ph.D. in clinical and community psychology from the University of Rochester. Dr. Jason is a former president of the Division of Community Psychology of the American Psychological Association and a past editor of *The Community Psychologist*. He has published more than 275 articles and chapters on preventive school-based interventions; the prevention of alcohol, tobacco, and other drug abuse; media interventions; and program evaluation. Dr. Jason has been on the editorial boards of seven psychological journals, and he has edited or written ten other books. He has served on review committees of the National Institute of Drug Abuse and the National Institute of Mental Health and has received more than $6 million in federal grants to support his research. Dr. Jason has received three media awards from the American Psychological Association, and he is frequently asked to comment on policy issues for numerous media outlets.

MARA B. ADELMAN (Ph.D., University of Washington) is an Assistant Professor in the Department of Communication at Seattle University. Her primary research is on social support networks and community integration that spans both intimate and nonintimate relationships. She studies these processes in specific contexts, including dating services and residential facilities. She is coauthor of *Communicating Social Support* (1997) and *The Fragile Community: Living Together With AIDS* (1997) and co-produced an ethnographic documentary video about Bonaventure House, entitled *The Pilgrim Must Embark: Living in Community*. She strongly believes that we need to take superficial relationships seriously in reclaiming our sense of community.

PATRICIA A. FENNELL, CSW-R, founder and director of Albany Health Management Associates, Inc. (AHMA) in Albany, New York, is nationally recognized as an author and the developer of an innovative, integrated psycho-social approach for the treatment of physical illness and trauma. She is an expert on recovery and has an extensive background in the treatment of chronic and terminal illness, sexual abuse, trauma syndromes, and Chronic Fatigue Syndrome. Ms. Fennell has served as consultant, lecturer, and keynote speaker to numerous national and regional mental and physical health organizations, HMOs, task forces, academic institutions, court systems, and pastoral care institutions. Together with her clinical team, she has provided ongoing treatment for hundreds of patients with chronic illness. In 1990 Ms. Fennell affiliated with the Capital Region Sleep Disorders Center of Albany Medical Center and St. Peter's Hospital in Albany, New York, for which she is currently a senior clinical consultant. Presently, she is a principal investigator of a joint Sleep Center and AHMA project examining sleep quality and the impact of the illness experience in patients with Chronic Fatigue Syndrome.

LAWRENCE R. FREY (Ph.D., University of Kansas) is a Professor in the Communication Department at Loyola University in Chicago. His research is designed to help revitalize the study of small group communications by demonstrating the applied value of research to real-life groups and encouraging the use of naturalistic research methods. Author or editor of six books (including *The Fragile Community: Living Together with AIDS*, with Mara B. Adelman) and 35 chapters and journal articles, his edited text *Group Communication in Context: Studies of Natural Groups* (1994), received both the 1995 Gerald R. Miller Award for outstanding scholarship and the 1994 Applied Communication Distinguished Book Award from the Speech Communication Association. He is the lead author of two quantitative methods textbooks adopted at 135 universities and a forthcoming textbook on qualitative methods. Dr. Frey serves as an associate editor on seven editorial boards and as a consulting reviewer for numerous journals. In 1983, he received the Outstanding Young Teacher Award from the Central States Communication Association; he is the current President-Elect of that association.

JOHN MORITSUGU is a Professor of Psychology at Pacific Lutheran University in Tacoma, Washington. He has been active in community psychology for many years, serving the American Psychological Association as National Coordinator of Regions, Chair of the Committee on Ethnic Minority Issues, and Representative to the APA Council for Division 27 (APA Society for Community Research and Action). He has also served as Co-President for Division 45 (APA Society for the Psychological Study of Ethnic Minority Issues) and as a member of the APA Board of Educational Affairs. He is presently Vice-President of the Asian-American Psychological Association. He was coeditor of the texts *Preventive Psychology* and *Prevention: Toward a Multidisciplinary Approach.*

CPSIA information can be obtained
at www.ICGtesting.com
Printed in the USA
BVHW042058020422
633207BV00002B/2

9 780275 958725